T0209722

An Analysis of

Claude Lévi-Strauss's

Structural
Anthropology

Kitty Wheater

Published by Macat International Ltd
24:13 Coda Centre, 189 Munster Road, London SW6 6AW.

Distributed exclusively by Routledge
2 Park Square, Milton Park, Abingdon, Oxon OX14 4RN
711 Third Avenue, New York, NY 10017, USA

Routledge is an imprint of the Taylor & Francis Group, an informa business

www.macat.com
info@macat.com

Cataloguing in Publication Data
A catalogue record for this book is available from the British Library.
Library of Congress Cataloguing-in-Publication Data is available upon request.
Cover illustration: Etienne Gilfillan

ISBN 978-1-912302-09-3 (hardback)
ISBN 978-1-912127-14-6 (paperback)
ISBN 978-1-912128-34-1 (e-book)

Notice
The information in this book is designed to orientate readers of the work under analysis,
to elucidate and contextualise its key ideas and themes, and to aid in the development
of critical thinking skills. It is not meant to be used, nor should it be used, as a
substitute for original thinking or in place of original writing or research. References and
notes are provided for informational purposes and their presence does not constitute
endorsement of the information or opinions therein. This book is presented solely for
educational purposes. It is sold on the understanding that the publisher is not engaged
to provide any scholarly advice. The publisher has made every effort to ensure that
this book is accurate and up-to-date, but makes no warranties or representations with
regard to the completeness or reliability of the information it contains. The information
and the opinions provided herein are not guaranteed or warranted to produce particular
results and may not be suitable for students of every ability. The publisher shall not be
liable for any loss, damage or disruption arising from any errors or omissions, or from
the use of this book, including, but not limited to, special, incidental, consequential or
other damages caused, or alleged to have been caused, directly or indirectly, by the
information contained within.

CONTENTS

THE MACAT LIBRARY

The Macat Library is a series of unique academic explorations of seminal works in the humanities and social sciences – books and papers that have had a significant and widely recognised impact on their disciplines. It has been created to serve as much more than just a summary of what lies between the covers of a great book. It illuminates and explores the influences on, ideas of, and impact of that book. Our goal is to offer a learning resource that encourages critical thinking and fosters a better, deeper understanding of important ideas.

Each publication is divided into three Sections: Influences, Ideas, and Impact. Each Section has four Modules. These explore every important facet of the work, and the responses to it.

This Section-Module structure makes a Macat Library book easy to use, but it has another important feature. Because each Macat book is written to the same format, it is possible (and encouraged!) to cross-reference multiple Macat books along the same lines of inquiry or research. This allows the reader to open up interesting interdisciplinary pathways.

To further aid your reading, lists of glossary terms and people mentioned are included at the end of this book (these are indicated by an asterisk [*] throughout) – as well as a list of works cited.

Macat has worked with the University of Cambridge to identify the elements of critical thinking and understand the ways in which six different skills combine to enable effective thinking.
Three allow us to fully understand a problem; three more give us the tools to solve it. Together, these six skills make up the **PACIER** model of critical thinking. They are:

ANALYSIS – understanding how an argument is built
EVALUATION – exploring the strengths and weaknesses of an argument
INTERPRETATION – understanding issues of meaning

CREATIVE THINKING – coming up with new ideas and fresh connections
PROBLEM-SOLVING – producing strong solutions
REASONING – creating strong arguments

To find out more, visit **WWW.MACAT.COM.**

CRITICAL THINKING AND *STRUCTURAL ANTHROPOLOGY*

Primary critical thinking skill: INTERPRETATION
Secondary critical thinking skill: CREATIVE THINKING

Claude Lévi-Strauss is probably the most complex anthropological theorist of all time. His work continues to influence present-day thinkers in his field, but he is perhaps even more influential beyond it. As one of the key figures in the development of what is known today as 'French theory,' Lévi-Strauss was one of the most important thinkers of the 20th-century.

His theories of interpretation, meaning and culture have helped shape the ideas and methodologies of a range of disciplines, above all literature and philosophy. At the heart of Lévi-Strauss's work are the questions of meaning and where meaning comes from. As an anthropologist, he was primarily interested in what completely different and separate cultures might have in common. Crucially, he saw how common ground resides not on the surface of cultures (i.e., in similar customs), but deep inside invisible background structures of thought. His quest was to peel away the surface of different cultures through careful interpretation, advancing from one layer to another until he discovered the structures that lay behind all of the exterior practices and meanings. Infamously challenging, his work shows interpretative skills working at the highest, most abstract level possible.

ABOUT THE AUTHOR OF THE ORIGINAL WORK

Claude Lévi-Strauss was a renowned French anthropologist, born into a secular Jewish family in 1908. He first studied philosophy, but was inspired to pursue his life's work after doing field research among native peoples in the Amazon during a four-year professorship in Brazil. Lévi-Strauss's cultural world view expanded further during World War II, when he fled France and became part of the scholarly community in New York City. After noticing patterns across the societies he knew—as well as others—he was the first person to develop the idea of structuralism in anthropology. Structuralism, said Lévi-Strauss, was based around the idea that all cultures have organizing principles that are connected. He died in Paris in 2009, at the age of 100.

ABOUT THE AUTHOR OF THE ANALYSIS

Kitty Wheater is a DPhil candidate in anthropology at the University of Oxford.

ABOUT MACAT

GREAT WORKS FOR CRITICAL THINKING

Macat is focused on making the ideas of the world's great thinkers accessible and comprehensible to everybody, everywhere, in ways that promote the development of enhanced critical thinking skills.

It works with leading academics from the world's top universities to produce new analyses that focus on the ideas and the impact of the most influential works ever written across a wide variety of academic disciplines. Each of the works that sit at the heart of its growing library is an enduring example of great thinking. But by setting them in context – and looking at the influences that shaped their authors, as well as the responses they provoked – Macat encourages readers to look at these classics and game-changers with fresh eyes. Readers learn to think, engage and challenge their ideas, rather than simply accepting them.

'Macat offers an amazing first-of-its-kind tool for interdisciplinary learning and research. Its focus on works that transformed their disciplines and its rigorous approach, drawing on the world's leading experts and educational institutions, opens up a world-class education to anyone.'

Andreas Schleicher
Director for Education and Skills, Organisation for Economic
Co-operation and Development

'Macat is taking on some of the major challenges in university education … They have drawn together a strong team of active academics who are producing teaching materials that are novel in the breadth of their approach.'

Prof Lord Broers,
former Vice-Chancellor of the University of Cambridge

'The Macat vision is exceptionally exciting. It focuses upon new modes of learning which analyse and explain seminal texts which have profoundly influenced world thinking and so social and economic development. It promotes the kind of critical thinking which is essential for any society and economy.
This is the learning of the future.'

Rt Hon Charles Clarke, former UK Secretary of State for Education

'The Macat analyses provide immediate access to the critical conversation surrounding the books that have shaped their respective discipline, which will make them an invaluable resource to all of those, students and teachers, working in the field.'

Professor William Tronzo, University of California at San Diego

WAYS IN TO THE TEXT

KEY POINTS

- Claude Lévi-Strauss was a pioneering French anthropologist* of the twentieth and early twenty-first centuries whose work on the fundamental structure and comparison of human societies made significant and lasting contributions to an understanding of humankind. Anthropology* is the study of human social and cultural life.

- In *Structural Anthropology* (originally published in French in 1958), Lévi-Strauss put forward a new anthropological world view, coming to the conclusion that different cultures* tend to share certain defining features.

- *Structural Anthropology* continues to be a central text in anthropology, living on as a landmark of thought and theory.

Who Was Claude Lévi-Strauss?

Claude Lévi-Strauss, the author of *Structural Anthropology*, was a French anthropologist born in Brussels, Belgium, in 1908. He pioneered the theoretical approach in anthropology known as structuralism,* which holds that all cultures have certain organizing principles in common, and that cultures must be understood in their relation to these universal structures. Lévi-Strauss also made enduring contributions that helped to shape the discipline of anthropology.

Lévi-Strauss grew up in Paris as part of a secular Jewish family. As a youth he was surrounded by artists and thinkers and gained exposure to the ideas of the nineteenth-century political philosopher Karl Marx* and to the work of Sigmund Freud,*⁸ the founder of the therapeutic and theoretical model of psychoanalysis.*¹ In 1931, Lévi-Strauss passed the French *agrégation** in philosophy*—a civil service test that qualified him to teach in the French public education system. After teaching for a few years, in 1935 he accepted a position as a visiting professor at a university in Brazil. During his four years in the country he briefly studied several tribes in the rain forest. It was a life-changing experience that exposed him to the ideas that would shape his career.

Not long after Lévi-Strauss returned to France, World War II* interrupted his life, forcing him to leave France after 1940. But it also thrust him in new and important directions. Unable to return to Brazil, Lévi-Strauss found refuge in New York City at the New School for Social Research* (now a college known as the New School), which invited him to teach a course based on his experiences in South America. While in Brazil, Lévi-Strauss had collected ethnographic* data—the scientific description of the customs of individual people and cultures—and his analysis of this data would transform not only his own career, but also the field of anthropology. In New York, Lévi-Strauss got to know the linguist Roman Jakobson,* whose work would inspire him.

What Does *Structural Anthropology* Say?
First published in France in 1958, *Structural Anthropology* is a collection of works written by Lévi-Strauss between 1944 and 1957. The pioneering book set the foundations for the field of structural anthropology, outlining an approach to the study of human societies still relevant today.

Structural anthropology is a school of anthropological thought that believes all cultures are linked by deep, unchanging structures. These structures, Lévi-Strauss argues, are common to all human minds, across different cultures. Conscious and unconscious, these underlying structures define how humans organize the world around them. They also set the basic patterns that develop into complex, diverse cultures. In Lévi-Strauss's view, cultures that seem extremely different, and which have different institutions and views, nonetheless have common structuring principles at their bases. When analyzed at a deep level, these common structures can be revealed. This in turn can expose crucial common elements of humanity in people who belong to radically different societies.

Overall, the volume makes a case for using these structuralist assumptions in investigating and comparing human societies, communities, and behavior. This leads to the belief that each cultural practice (such as marriage, for instance) has a similarly structured counterpart in some other culture. It also means that at the most fundamental level all cultures are equivalent. They can, and should, therefore, be compared and analyzed so as to reveal the structures they have in common. Lévi-Strauss makes the case for this analytical practice by exploring case studies that rely on examples drawn from various premodern* culture groups spread across the world.

It is important to note that *Structural Anthropology* is a complicated text. Indeed, it is famously challenging to read and understand, reflecting the nature of Lévi-Strauss himself. Trained in several linked fields, he was as much a philosopher as he was an anthropologist.

More than this, though, *Structural Anthropology*'s very complexity is also a key part of the argument it makes. In an effort to find the deepest levels of common mental structure across humankind, Lévi-Strauss works at a highly abstract level of understanding. Searching structures that create a framework for human culture, he is constantly looking for unconscious thought processes. He delves further into the abstract realm by searching for systems by which the unconscious thought processes interact with and relate to each other. For Lévi-Strauss, a structure is a deeply rooted, unchangeable element that cannot be seen—and which is hard even to describe. He believes these structures are the equivalent of genetic material—the tiny building blocks of living cells through which each generation inherits from the one before. But instead of creating cells or tissue, the structures create the founding principles of human culture. The heart of the book is Lévi-Strauss's attempts to trace, outline, and explain these hidden structures.

Why Does *Structural Anthropology* Matter?

Lévi-Strauss has been called one of the "fathers" of modern anthropology.[2] *Structural Anthropology* remains a fundamentally important text for anyone examining how we might best understand human culture and behavior.

Lévi-Strauss's landmark work remains influential more than half a century after publication, even though not everyone accepts all the arguments it makes.[3] But even for those who dispute the use of the structural approach, the text is too important to be discarded. It is an essential part of decades of discussion and scholarship.

Structural Anthropology's influence also extends far beyond anthropology. Claude Lévi-Strauss's structuralist theory is widely considered to be one of the most important schools of thought in other disciplines in the period following World War II. In France, for much of the 1950s and 1960s structuralism dominated the humanities* (the multiple disciplines—such as literature, art, and music—that study how humans express themselves) and the social sciences* (such as economics, politics, and history). Many of the theoretical movements that came later are defined by structuralism. Crucial figures in theory and philosophy were profoundly influenced by Lévi-Strauss's work, including the literary theorist Roland Barthes* and the philosophers Julia Kristeva* and Jacques Derrida.*

The work remains important in spite of critics[4] and detractors because it is a monumental example of the ongoing (and never-ending) anthropological inquiry that seeks to answer the essential questions:

- What makes humans human?
- How do cultures function?
- Can we reach an understanding of culture and of ourselves by observing and comparing one group of humans with another group?

Lévi-Strauss's intellectual quest was in the end as much about philosophy as it was about anthropology. He sought the basic structures that form the essential framework of human culture, and tried to find examples of similarities across time and space.

NOTES

1   "Lévi-Strauss, Claude," in Claire Smith, ed., *Encyclopedia of Global Archaeology* (New York: Springer-Verlag, 2014), 4506–8.

2   Patrick Wilcken, *Claude Lévi-Strauss: The Father of Modern Anthropology* (London: Penguin, 2010). The reference to his being the father of anthropology is in the book's title.

3   Robert Crosby, "Structuralism and Lévi-Strauss," *The Harvard Crimson,* November 17, 1970, accessed September 5, 2015, http://www.thecrimson.com/article/1970/11/17/structuralism-and-levi-strauss-pin-the-last/.

4   Simon Clarke, *The Foundations of Structuralism: A Critique of Lévi-Strauss and the Structuralist Movement* (Brighton, Sussex: Harvester Press; Totowa, NJ: Barnes & Noble, 1981).

SECTION 1
INFLUENCES

MODULE 1
THE AUTHOR AND THE HISTORICAL CONTEXT

KEY POINTS

- *Structural Anthropology* is one of the twentieth century's most influential works in the social sciences* (a collection of academic disciplines encompassing anthropology,* economics, geography, history, political science, and sociology*).

- The life experiences of Claude Lévi-Strauss in France, Brazil, and the United States shaped his thinking about culture.*

- Lévi-Strauss argued that human culture groups were linked to each other by basic, unchanging structures.

Why Read This Text?

Claude Lévi-Strauss, the author of *Structural Anthropology*, originally printed as *Anthropologie Structurale* in 1958, was a faculty member of the prestigious École Pratique des Hautes Études* in Paris when the work was published. The English translation appeared five years later.[1] This volume focused on the doctrine of structuralism,* according to which all cultures have certain organizing principles in common, and must, then, be understood in their relation to these universal structures. Lévi-Strauss sought to combine the techniques of linguistics* (the study of language) with his own ethnographic* studies of human culture groups; "ethnography" refers to written texts containing the findings and analysis of anthropological study. He saw many parallels between the patterns that govern speech and those that govern culture, focusing especially on kinship* (social ties), myth* (roughly, traditional stories), and art.

> ❝ ... I don't have the feeling that I write my books.
> I have the feeling that my books get written through
> me ... Each of us is a kind of crossroads where things
> happen. The crossroads is purely passive ... there is no
> choice, it is just a matter of chance. ❞
>
> Claude Lévi-Strauss, radio interview with the Canadian Broadcasting
> Company, 1977

In Lévi-Strauss's view, ideas about cultures evolving in a manner similar to biological evolution* were insufficient.[2] As he observed and compared cultures, he sought universal elements that were similar to the basic units of language, grammar, and pronunciation. He believed that by reducing culture to abstract elements, he could then establish and examine relationships between those elements.[3]

Structural Anthropology presents the arc of Lévi-Strauss's thinking across the 1940s and 1950s. With its publication the text sparked great debate that continues today, since the school of poststructural* thought—an approach to the analysis of culture that questions things such as the security of objective* truth—is defined by its opposition to the ideas of Lévi-Strauss and others.[4] Structuralism, along with its intellectual descendants and even its opponents, seeks to understand the most fundamental elements of human culture and, in this way, understand the actions and interactions of humans themselves.[5] Although much criticized and frequently dense, *Structural Anthropology* remains one of the key works of social theory produced during the twentieth century. It has profoundly influenced the development of the humanities* (academic disciplines that study human culture, including politics, history, and literature) and social sciences since the 1970s.

Author's Life

Lévi-Strauss attended prestigious lycées (the equivalent of high schools) in Paris and, later, the Université Paris-Sorbonne,* a public research university, studying law and philosophy* there. In 1935 he served as a visiting professor of sociology (the study of social structures and social behavior) at the University of São Paulo, Brazil. Together with his wife, Dina Lévi-Strauss, he conducted fieldwork* between 1935 and 1939, collecting ethnographic (that is, firsthand, cultural) data on several indigenous* (native) tribes, including the Guaycuru,* Bororo,* Nambikwara,* and Tupi-Kawahib,* during expeditions to the Amazon rain forest.

After being exiled from France because the Vichy* (pro-German) government established anti-Jewish laws in 1940, Lévi-Strauss accepted a post at the New School for Social Research* (now the New School) in New York City, teaching courses based on his experiences in South America. New York's intellectual culture introduced him to other influential thinkers—including non-French thinkers. Lévi-Strauss's relationship with the structural linguist* Roman Jakobson* proved influential. In Jakobson's approach to the study of language Lévi-Strauss encountered a means of analyzing the structural framework of human culture, kinship, and myth.

In 1947 Lévi-Strauss returned to the Sorbonne, completing his doctorate in 1948.[6] He published the influential *Tristes Tropiques* (*The Sad Tropics*) in 1955. After *Structural Anthropology* appeared, Lévi-Strauss continued to produce influential theory, most notably *La Pensée sauvage* (*The Savage Mind*) in 1962 (with the English translation in 1966). In 1973, Lévi-Strauss was elected to the Académie Française,* the highest civic recognition a French writer can receive.[7] He was praised by the same body on reaching his 100th birthday.[8] Lévi-Strauss died on October 30, 2009, a month before he would have turned 101.

Author's Background

The life and intellectual career of Claude Lévi-Strauss coincided with a period of massive global change. World War II,* the Holocaust* (the systematic murder of millions of Jews and other persecuted minorities by the extreme right-wing regime of Nazi* Germany), the postwar decline of European society, and the rise in the importance of the United States all affected Lévi-Strauss and the world in which he lived. These epic changes are to be found in virtually every area of life—technology, science, medicine, geopolitics—and their cumulative effect is hard to judge. What is clear is that the course of the twentieth century radically altered the human experience—sometimes in positive ways, other times not. Technological and economic globalization* (the growing influence of ties, influences, and connections across continental borders) were forces that appeared to strip away the unique features of cultures and societies. This march of "progress" appeared to have a blurring effect between cultures. It created a questioning intellectual environment, in which Lévi-Strauss sought the essential building blocks of humanity by studying premodern,* nonindustrialized people.

NOTES

1 Claude Lévi-Strauss, *Structural Anthropology*, trans. Claire Jacobson and Brooke Grundfest Schoepf (New York: Basic Books, 1963).

2 Lévi-Strauss, *Structural Anthropology*, 7–8.

3 Lévi-Strauss, *Structural Anthropology*, 12.

4 Paul Harrison, "Post-structural Theories," in *Approaches to Human Geography*, ed. S. Aitken and G. Valentine (London: Sage, 2006): 122–35.

5 Chris Y. Tilley, "Claude Lévi-Strauss: Structuralism and Beyond," in *Reading Material Culture*, ed. C. Y. Tilley (Cambridge, MA: Blackwell, 1990): 3–81.

6 Claude Lévi-Strauss, *La Vie familiale et sociale des indiens Nambikwara* (Paris: Au siège de la société, Musée de l'Homme, 1948), and Claude Lévi-Strauss, *The Elementary Structures of Kinship* (Boston, MA: Beacon Press, 1969).

7   Académie Française, "Claude Lévi-Strauss," accessed November 1, 2015, http://www.academie-francaise.fr/les-immortels/claude-levi-strauss.

8   Hélène Carrère-d'Encausse, "Adresse à M. le professeur Claude Lévi-Strauss à l'occasion de son centième anniversaire," accessed November 1, 2015, http://www.academie-francaise.fr/adresse-m-le-professeur-claude-levi-strauss-loccasion-de-son-centieme-anniversaire.

MODULE 2
ACADEMIC CONTEXT

KEY POINTS

- *Structural Anthropology* contributed to the growth of anthropology* in the twentieth century, as well as influencing contemporary French thought.
- An international range of scholars influenced Claude Lévi-Strauss during his exile from France in the 1940s.
- Lévi-Strauss applied methods borrowed from linguistics* (the study of language) to create a novel approach to anthropological inquiry.

The Work in Its Context

Claude Lévi-Strauss's *Structural Anthropology* played an important role in the development of the social sciences.* Lévi-Strauss argued strongly that anthropology and sociology* are separate branches of knowledge, and his study makes original contributions to the emergence of anthropology as its own discipline.

In *Structural Anthropology* Lévi-Strauss is able to identify and describe a number of key elements across cultures,* aided by his time spent in Brazil and the United States after he was forced to leave France. These cross-cultural points of view led him in *Structural Anthropology* to identify and analyze globalizing* elements of human culture that argue for cultural similarity and closeness ("globalization" refers to the process by which cultures become more alike and more connected, driven by technology and by increasing economic ties among nations). Lévi-Strauss also gained perspective from colleagues whose work he encountered; his existence as an exile from his homeland yielded opportunities.

> ❝ When one confines oneself to the study of a single society, one may do valuable work. ❞
>
> Claude Lévi-Strauss, *Structural Anthropology*

In New York he met fellow refugee Roman Jakobson,* a Russian American structural linguist* (structural linguistics treats language as a structure in which the meaning of every element is affected by its relationship to other parts of the language). Jakobson had an interest in semiotics*—the study of signs and symbols—and applied the methods of the Swiss semiotician Ferdinand de Saussure* to linguistics in a novel manner, searching for the smallest building blocks of language. Jakobson influenced Lévi-Strauss in profound ways. In 1945, Lévi-Strauss published *L'Analyse structurale en linguistique et en anthropologie*[1] ("Structural Analysis in Linguistics and Anthropology," later the second chapter of *Structural Anthropology*), in which he applied Jakobson's techniques to other forms of culture, especially kinship.*

Overview of the Field

Claude Lévi-Strauss believed that an anthropologist must collect evidence by means of direct observation, through fieldwork* (research in the field).[2] He based this idea, at least in part, on his admiration for the work of the German American anthropologist Franz Boas.* In the early days of Lévi-Strauss's career, sociology was a more dominant and widely studied discipline than anthropology. The pioneering work of Boas, as well as that of Polish anthropologist Bronisław Malinowski,* showed that firsthand ethnographic* observation was the key to creating reliable microhistories of a sample population of limited size;[3] "microhistory" here simply refers to a study restricted to a specific time and place. Lévi-Strauss tried to follow this model in his own ethnographic observations of kinship models in the Americas, an approach that would remain with him even as he progressed during his career from a junior researcher to an established academic anthropologist.

When Lévi-Strauss's work began to gain exposure, he received initial, positive reactions from the French philosopher Simone de Beauvoir* in *Les Temps Modernes*, a monthly literary review started by the philosopher Jean-Paul Sartre.* Both Lévi-Strauss and Sartre lived at a time when intellectuals reacted against the perceived faults of the French government.[4] For Lévi-Strauss this time of difficulty in France served to underscore his belief that European perspectives had been overemphasized by social scientists and philosophers, and that this focus on European thought made it harder to understand the place of humankind in the world more clearly.

Academic Influences

Structural Anthropology was published at a key point in the development of the discipline of anthropology in France, a process that was certainly affected by the intellectual climate, academic disruption, and consequences of World Wars I* and II.* Claude Lévi-Strauss's novel theoretical approach to anthropology, demonstrated by his structural analysis of human culture in *Structural Anthropology*, put anthropology on the intellectual map in France. Lévi-Strauss was influenced by several French predecessors, notably the philosopher and sociologist Émile Durkheim* and the sociologist Marcel Mauss,* Durkheim's nephew.

Durkheim, a pioneer of sociology, argued that individual assumptions, behavior, and motivation were conditioned by what he called "social facts"*—cultural norms and social structures that exercised influence and power above and beyond an individual's agency* (that is, a person's ability to act effectively).[5] Durkheim founded the journal *L'Année Sociologique* in 1898 to raise the profile of sociology in France. The journal particularly influenced Lévi-Strauss, as did the work of Mauss, the author of *The Gift* (1925)—a landmark study of gift exchange as an essential feature of both primitive and developed societies.

Along with these French influences, Lévi-Strauss would also gain perspectives during his wartime exile in the United States, where he came into contact both with structural linguistics, and also with Jakobson and the community of American cultural anthropology. Just as twentieth-century globalization directed Lévi-Strauss's interests toward the essential elements of human society and culture, so the range of intellectual influences behind *Structural Anthropology* demonstrates the effect of globalization upon Lévi-Strauss himself.

NOTES

1   Claude Lévi-Strauss, "Structural Analysis in Linguistics and in Anthropology," *Word* 1, no. 2 (1945): 1–12.

2   Claude Lévi-Strauss, *Structural Anthropology*, trans. Claire Jacobson and Brooke Grundfest Schoepf (New York: Basic Books, 1963), 8–9.

3   Lévi-Strauss, *Structural Anthropology*, 14–15.

4   See Henry Stuart Hughes, *The Obstructed Path: French Social Thought in the Years of Desperation, 1930–1960* (New Jersey: Harper & Row, 1968).

5   David Émile Durkheim, *The Division of Labour in Society*, trans. Lewis A. Coser (New York: The Free Press, 1984).

MODULE 3
THE PROBLEM

KEY POINTS

- Claude Lévi-Strauss advocates a need for close observation of cultural groups in order to understand humankind better.

- *Structural Anthropology* presents a theoretically informed analysis based on linguistics* (the study of language) and ethnography* (written records of anthropological study).

- Lévi-Strauss argued that anthropologists can analyze culture* in the same way structural linguists* analyze language—by making an analysis of the structural elements that, related as part of a system, serve to define it.

Core Question

In *Structural Anthropology*, Claude Lévi-Strauss addressed three fundamental questions in anthropology:*

- Where do human cultures come from?
- What do they have in common?
- Why do they have these things in common?

By using the word "structural," Lévi-Strauss reveals that he will employ a particular theoretical framework; by referring to "anthropology," he consciously departs from the more common approaches of sociology* and ethnology* (a somewhat obsolete term for a branch of anthropology in which ethnographic data is compared in order to make comparisons of different cultures).

Lévi-Strauss considers humankind in terms of its structure, seeking to reduce social and cultural institutions* such as the family and belief

❝ A truly scientific analysis must be real, simplifying, and explanatory. ❞

Claude Lévi-Strauss, *Structural Anthropology*

to abstract elements, and then to observe the relationships between those elements. He feels strongly that scientific interpretations should be both *simplifying*, which enables cross-cultural comparison, and *explanatory*, within the unique framework of a given society.[1]

Structural Anthropology applies the methods of linguistics to kinship* studies, which are interested in understanding the social life of blood relationships by studying ancestry and marriage customs. Kinship terms* have a twofold purpose—they are both sociological* constructions and speech acts.

The word "brother," for example, has a specific definition that society has agreed on (it is a "sociological construction"), but when used in speech "brother" can imply meanings that go beyond the literal definition.

Human kinship systems perform several different social functions, ranging from identifying family relationships to defining appropriate behavior;[2] Lévi-Strauss argues that all cultures possess a system of terminology (the vocabulary of family—"mother," "sister," and so on) and a system of psychological* and social attitudes, according to which we behave differently toward different people according to the nature of our kinship. These terms and attitudes must be acknowledged if we are to analyze kinship.

Each system presents its own challenges, as far as the methods of research and analysis are concerned. As a result they must be approached separately.[3]

In short, Lévi-Strauss seeks to discover the subtle functioning of kinship by reducing the behaviors of humankind to their most fundamental elements.

The Participants

The debate about the structure of human kinship and society had begun prior to Lévi-Strauss. The British anthropologist Alfred Radcliffe-Brown,* influenced by the pioneering sociologist Émile Durkheim,* saw institutions (which include things such as kinship) as an essential element for maintaining social order. For him, these institutions helped keep societies running well and adapting to change as necessary.

Radcliffe-Brown and Lévi-Strauss agreed in some areas, but Radcliffe-Brown made a distinction between social structures and social relations.

For Lévi-Strauss, social structures were the key to life in society; for Radcliffe-Brown, they were a scientist's theoretical observation: social relations were real.[4] Radcliffe-Brown felt that social anthropology had not yet reached the level of being a "formed science."[5] Radcliffe-Brown and Lévi-Strauss also disagreed on the mechanisms of social evolution* and change. Radcliffe-Brown argued that primitive, tribal societies were each at various stages along a predictable path toward cultural and social progress, while Lévi-Strauss thought that similarities and differences between tribal groups could be explained by reconstructing the ways the tribes had interacted.[6]

The Austrian American anthropologist Robert Lowie,* a student of the highly influential German American anthropologist Franz Boas,* influenced Lévi-Strauss's work by developing a four-part classification system for kinship analysis. Lowie took the emphasis off cultural evolution, believing it suggested that some cultures were better or "more developed" than others, in favor of cultural relativism.* The idea behind cultural relativism is that specific beliefs or behaviors are best understood in terms of their function within their own culture, and should not be judged according to the world view or moral standards of the external onlooker.[7] Lowie argued that cultures were always changing within themselves, while acknowledging that change can happen because culture groups interact with each other.

The Contemporary Debate

A key contemporary debate that shaped both Lévi-Strauss and his social-scientific peers concerned whether history or science was better suited to uncovering the "truth" about human societies and cultures.

History was considered to be the study of what was meaningful to human beings; science, the study of what was objectively*—accurately and impartially—observable, regardless of its human meaning. Franz Boas was central to this debate, which had its roots in nineteenth-century German academia.

Boas had begun his life as a student of physics, and some believed that he used the rigorous scientific methods* of the physicist as a platform for his work in anthropology. Others, however, contended that Boas had "rejected" physics in favor of history. In Lévi-Strauss's case, the decision to adopt the structural linguistic* methods of the Russian American scholar Roman Jakobson* seems "scientific," in that this approach is concerned with determining the status of fundamental elements of social institutions.

Boas's school of thought influenced Lévi-Strauss at a key moment: for Boas, although anthropology includes a historical sensibility, it was also a science because it was based on empiricism*—arriving at knowledge through facts verifiable by observation. Anthropology, according to Boas, should gather knowledge based on firsthand observation and experience, rather than simply using untested assumptions generated from abstract theories or secondary sources. He believed it should incorporate cultural and historical context in describing observable social interactions.

NOTES

1   Claude Lévi-Strauss, *Structural Anthropology*, trans. Claire Jacobson and Brooke Grundfest Schoepf (New York: Basic Books, 1963), 35.

2   Lévi-Strauss, *Structural Anthropology*, 37.

3   Lévi-Strauss, *Structural Anthropology*, 37.

4   A. R. Radcliffe-Brown, "On Social Structure," *Journal of the Royal Anthropological Institute of Great Britain and Ireland* 70, no.1 (1940): 1–12.

5   Radcliffe-Brown, "On Social Structure," 3.

6   A. R. Radcliffe-Brown, "The Comparative Method in Social Anthropology," *Journal of the Royal Anthropological Institute of Great Britain and Ireland* 81, no. 1/2 (1951): 15–22.

7   Robert H. Lowie, *Primitive Society* (New York: Liveright Pub. Corp., 1947).

THE AUTHOR'S CONTRIBUTION

KEY POINTS

- Lévi-Strauss advanced a new way of thinking about humankind and its cultural institutions* (norms and subsystems such as kinship*) in *Structural Anthropology*.

- Lévi-Strauss observed that data reveal the presence of numerous binary oppositions,* or choices between two opposites, in human culture.*

- *Structural Anthropology* argues that culture and language function in similar ways and that linguistic* methods can be used to study cultural forces and change.

Author's Aims

In *Structural Anthropology*, Claude Lévi-Strauss aimed to show that human cultures can best be understood by comparing their underlying structures.[1] He wanted anthropology* to be considered a discipline that employed scientific methods* in a way that would distinguish it from sociology.* Lévi-Strauss adapted for his own purposes the methods of other disciplines, notably linguistics. His aim, overall, was to boil the cultures of humankind down to their most essential elements, some of which are so common and familiar as to be unconscious.[2] He believed the systems revealed by the relationships between these elements would yield a science of the universal nature of man.

Lévi-Strauss adopted an interest in binary opposition, or pairs of opposites, from earlier scholars who argued that opposition is the means by which expressions in language have value or meaning. Many aspects of human behavior, culture, and language can be discussed in

> **" If a myth is made up of all its variants, structural analysis should take all of them into account. "**
>
> Claude Lévi-Strauss, *Structural Anthropology*

terms of binary oppositions. Rather than being a contradictory relationship, the two opposites help explain each other.[3] In applying binary opposition to the study of structure in human cultures, Lévi-Strauss aimed to show that kinship systems, for example, could "be summarized in terms of five binary oppositions."[4] He argued that these oppositions determined marriage rules.

Approach

Lévi-Strauss blends together different approaches in *Structural Anthropology*. As a system of thought, structuralism* requires the study of empirical* data (information verifiable by observation), both social and cultural. In chapter 2, Lévi-Strauss applies this approach to kinship studies.

Some earlier anthropologists made the self-contained family unit the starting point of kinship analysis: husband, wife, and children. Lévi-Strauss looked instead to the types of relationship *between* families, to identify the structural elements of kinship. He identifies four relational terms (brother, sister, father, and son) that as a whole are the beginning of a system of kinship relations. He argues that kinship relations may ultimately be divided into two groups, which each represent two generations. One group describes blood relations— brother, sister, father, and son; the other describes ties established by marriage—maternal uncle, nephew, husband, and wife. Although Lévi-Strauss was later criticized for this male-centered model, he argued that "in human society it is the men who exchange the women, and not *vice versa*."[5]

In chapter 11 of *Structural Anthropology* Lévi-Strauss applies a similar approach to the study of myth* (bodies of traditional stories). The structural approach to myth involves realizing that the meaning of myth cannot lie in its elements alone, but only in the relation between the elements. Armed with the approaches of the structural linguists, Lévi-Strauss argued that "Myth is language, functioning on an especially high level." This was because the story told by the interrelating elements of myth makes it instantly recognizable as myth, regardless of the language in which it is expressed. This is different from poetry, for example, which would become unrecognizable were its style and word arrangement to change.[6] Lévi-Strauss argued that cross-cultural comparisons of the elements of myth were another key to understanding humankind. This supported his ultimate goal in *Structural Anthropology*—to demonstrate that seemingly unrelated human groups actually shared common structures.

Contribution in Context

Lévi-Strauss did not invent the idea of structuralism or the practice of kinship analysis. His work may, then, be seen as part of a series of related developments in the social sciences* during the nineteenth and twentieth centuries, all of which involve new methods of analyzing human behavior and institutions. In an effort to understand contemporary European and American culture better, social scientists used so-called "primitive" or premodern* cultures as a laboratory of sorts, from which to generate rules about the behaviors and cultures of humankind in general. This process can be said to have begun in the eighteenth century with the German philosopher Immanuel Kant,* one of the most influential thinkers in history, and the first to promote anthropology as a field worthy of intellectual study. Kant believed anthropology should include two categories: one that involved human physiology* (the study of how the body works), the other a practical examination of the things a human being "can and should make of himself."[7] Kant positioned humanity at the center of all knowledge-making—an important philosophical footing for the coming generations of anthropologists.[8]

Sociologists, ethnologists* (those engaged in the comparison of different cultures), and anthropologists in France, Germany, and the United States followed in the wake of Kant in the nineteenth and twentieth centuries. They differed from Kant in that they sought to understand their fields and subjects better through firsthand data collection—similar to how their colleagues in the physical sciences were collecting data in the laboratory.

Fieldwork* among the "primitive" tribes of the world provided the basis for intellectual advancement that continues today, and Lévi-Strauss played a key role in this effort. These contributions are significant regardless of their critical reception. In *Structural Anthropology* Lévi-Strauss is keenly aware of the need for anthropology to be an informed discipline in its own right, separate from sociology and ethnology.

When the Swiss linguist Ferdinand de Saussure* shaped the field of linguistics with his groundbreaking theoretical propositions of the early twentieth century, he wondered whether a science of language was even possible.[9] Lévi-Strauss followed a similar path, testing the ways in which anthropology might become more empirical and scientific.

NOTES

1   Claude Lévi-Strauss, *Structural Anthropology*, trans. Claire Jacobson and Brooke Grundfest Schoepf (New York: Basic Books, 1963), 30–1.

2   Lévi-Strauss. *Structural Anthropology*, 281–3.

3   Ferdinand de Saussure, Écrits de linguistique générale (Paris: Gallimard, 2002).

4   Lévi-Strauss, *Structural Anthropology*, 159.

5   Lévi-Strauss, *Structural Anthropology,* 49.

6   Lévi-Strauss, *Structural Anthropology*, 210.

7   Immanuel Kant, *Anthropology from a Pragmatic Point of View*, trans. V. L. Dodwell and H. H. Rudnick (Carbondale, IL: Southern Illinois University Press, 1978).

8   Michael Rohlf, "Immanuel Kant," in *Stanford Encyclopedia of Philosophy*, accessed February 1, 2016, http://plato.stanford.edu/entries/kant/.

9   Ferdinand de Saussure, *Course in General Linguistics,* trans. Roy Harris (London: Duckworth, 2013).

SECTION 2
IDEAS

MODULE 5
MAIN IDEAS

KEY POINTS

- *Structural Anthropology* examines the relationships, both conscious and unconscious, that form the structure of human cultures.*

- The structures of human thought and culture are based on a universal human tendency to observe binary oppositions* (pairs of opposites) in the world.

- Structures in religion and myth* define how humans view their world and organize their experiences.

Key Themes

Claude Lévi-Strauss's *Structural Anthropology* has two main themes, chief of which is the presentation of the "structural* method" of anthropology.* This method aims to discover structural constants in three areas: art, kinship* (as it relates to personal relationships, such as those defined by marriage bonds), and religion.[1] The second main theme is an effort to position the discipline of anthropology within the social sciences,* debating its relation to other fields of inquiry (such as sociology*) and suggesting ways in which the disciplinary framework should develop.

Structural analysis had previously been applied to linguistics,* the study of language. Lévi-Strauss, influenced by the Russian American linguist Roman Jakobson,* used linguistic methods to analyze human culture and society. Studies in linguistics show how the human mind distinguishes between phonemes,* the individual sounds that form the building blocks of speech. Lévi-Strauss believed that since binary oppositions exist both in phonemes and in kinship systems, then the

> ❝ So the conclusion which seems to me the most likely is that some kind of correlation exists between certain things on certain levels, and our main task is to determine what these things are and what these levels are. ❞
>
> Claude Lévi-Strauss, *Structural Anthropology*

same approach could be taken when studying human kinship. But he is careful to point out also that "the superficial analogy between phonemic systems and kinship systems is so strong" that there is a danger that this approach might immediately "[set] us on the wrong track."[2] It seems that even Lévi-Strauss wished to be cautious about oversimplifying, admitting that some elements of culture cannot be studied through structural analysis: it was not enough to study kinship terms* without a parallel analysis of how those terms were embodied by differences in behavior (we speak differently to our "mother" and to our "mother-in-law").

Exploring the Ideas

Lévi-Strauss establishes a cross-cultural framework in *Structural Anthropology* by carefully distinguishing historical studies from sociology, noting that sociological method is always comparative in its nature. Fortunately Lévi-Strauss had concrete data available for the analysis of myth and religion from this cross-cultural and structuralist point of view. He was fascinated by what he argued were common patterns in myth, observing "an astounding similarity between myths collected in widely different regions."[3]

Lévi-Strauss's analysis of the myth of the Greek king Oedipus* (chapter 12) shows his investigation of binary opposition in myth and ritual. Lévi-Strauss regards the Oedipus story as a cultural attempt to explain the differences between the *theory* of the origin of man (that humanity emerged "from one"—that Eve came from Adam's rib, for example, in the Christian and Jewish mythical tradition) with the *experience* that man is born "from two": a man and a woman. Myth is therefore a "logical tool"in which binary oppositions are used to produce some kind of resolution. [4]

For instance, Lévi-Strauss sees the central act of the Oedipus myth ("Oedipus kills his father")[5] as an instance of a frequent mythical feature: the hostile "underrating of blood relations," whereby—usually—family members kill each other.[6] The binary opposite, then, is the "overrating of blood relations," whereby blood relations are "more intimate than they should be."[7] Oedipus's marriage to his mother is one "overrating" feature, in binary opposition with the "underrating"of Oedipus's murder of his father.

For Lévi-Strauss, this binary opposition resembled the one about the "origins of man"—"one/same" against "two/different." This repeating structure, in Lévi-Strauss's view, helps to make the meaning of the myth more apparent. He concludes that "the overrating of blood relations is to the underrating of blood relations as the attempt to escape [the idea of single/same origin] is to the impossibility to succeed in it."[8] Perhaps it is not surprising that the British anthropologist Edmund Leach* pointedly comments, "all this is vaguely reminiscent of an argument from *Alice Through the Looking Glass,*"a fantasy novel by Lewis Carroll.* [9]

Language and Expression

Structural Anthropology is a challenging and often dense work of scholarship. The original work in French appeared in 1958, with an English translation following in 1963. Because of the complexity of the subject, there were challenges in translating the work from French to English, a circumstance predicted by Lévi-Strauss himself in the preface of the 1958 French edition.[10] *Structural Anthropology* assumes that the reader is familiar not only with Lévi-Strauss's previous work, but also with a wide range of basic work in sociology, linguistics, and ethnography.* Lévi-Strauss makes frequent reference to scholars and studies without much explanation, so the data and arguments he presents are challenging to the reader who is not already familiar with the topic.

The structure of the volume adds another challenge, because the 17 chapters were not composed as a single book, but rather represent scholarly work done over the course of more than a decade. The style and point of view of the writing shifts from time to time, as well. Readers of *Structural Anthropology* may find it difficult to understand the case studies Lévi-Strauss offers when describing structuralism,* because of unfamiliarity with the supporting evidence. The discussion of kinship that supports the analysis of binary oppositions in structuralist thinking requires a familiarity with the way that kinship structures are understood in the discipline of anthropology, with the differences between regional kinship rules, and, ideally, with marriage rules.[11]

As Edmund Leach noted, the difficulty of understanding the text, whether in English or French, represents one of its "outstanding characteristics."[12]

NOTES

1   Claude Lévi-Strauss. *Structural Anthropology*, trans. Claire Jacobson and Brooke Grundfest Schoepf (New York: Basic Books, 1963), 82.

2   Lévi-Strauss, *Structural Anthropology*, 35.

3   Lévi-Strauss, *Structural Anthropology*, 208.

4   Lévi-Strauss, *Structural Anthropology*, 216.

5   Lévi-Strauss, *Structural Anthropology*, 214.

6   Lévi-Strauss, *Structural Anthropology*, 215.

7   Lévi-Strauss, *Structural Anthropology*, 215.

8   Lévi-Strauss, *Structural Anthropology*, 216.

9   Edmund Leach, *Lévi-Strauss*, 1st edn (London: Fontana Press, 1970), 65.
    Lewis Carroll wrote *Alice's Adventures in Wonderland* (1865) and a sequel,
    Through the Looking-Glass, and What Alice Found There (1871). Leach was
    probably referring to the first, although the title he cites is a combination of
    the two.

10 Claude Lévi-Strauss, *Anthropologie structurale* (Paris: Plon, 1958), ⊢ıı.

11 Lévi-Strauss, *Structural Anthropology*, 158–61.

12 Edmund Leach, *Lévi-Strauss*, 4th edn (London: Fontana Press, 1996), 16.

MODULE 6
SECONDARY IDEAS

KEY POINTS

- The sheer number of ideas presented in *Structural Anthropology* adds to the difficulty of understanding the work.
- The use of "magic," in the form of casting out spells for healing purposes, occurs repeatedly across cultures.*
- Primitive art provides insight into the underlying culture, and can be used to identify similarities between cultures.

Other Ideas

Claude Lévi-Strauss expresses such a multitude of ideas and covers such extensive geographical and thematic ground in *Structural Anthropology*—from classical myth,* to social structure in contemporary Brazil, to the art of Asia—that it would be hard to list all of these briefly. Because the volume contains 17 separate papers, it is easy to get lost within this multitude of ideas and themes, and within Lévi-Strauss's own poetic language.

Nonetheless, a few themes deserve special attention: first, Lévi-Strauss makes a wholehearted move away from ideas of cultural "evolution."* In *Structural Anthropology*, his structural analysis of human social and cultural life demonstrates why cultural change is not similar to biological evolution. Second, despite his identification of particular structures in social and cultural life, Lévi-Strauss did not believe culture to be either stable or self-contained.[1] Evidence of cultural variation demonstrated the creativity of culture, even if it could be classified within particular fundamental structures. Third, Lévi-Strauss's interest in the "universal mind" (a phenomenon indicated by the existence of

> ❝ The genuinely valuable part of Lévi-Strauss's
> contribution, in my view [is] the truly poetic range of
> associations which he brings to bear in the course of his
> analysis. ❞
>
> Edmund Leach, *Lévi-Strauss*

social structures shared by different cultures) made him willing to expand anthropological study to include the more "individual" sciences of psychology* (study of the mind) and physiology* (study of the physical functions). This informed his analysis of magic and healing.

Finally, perhaps most importantly, Lévi-Strauss acknowledged that binary opposition* has shortcomings as an analytical tool, paving the way for poststructural* approaches in anthropology* (poststructuralism is an approach noted for things such as the challenge it presents to secure and objective* notions of "truth").

Exploring the Ideas

Lévi-Strauss's structuralism* was a definite move away from the ideas of cultural "evolution" that lingered into the mid-twentieth century in anthropology. He argued that structural comparison demonstrated consistent rules, true for different cultures, governing the construction of social institutions and cultural things such as kinship* or myth. This showed that, fundamentally, cultures were more alike than they were different. By contrast, a focus on cultural evolution led to some cultures being considered "more evolved" than others. This had caused previous anthropologists to rank cultures separately, and was ultimately incompatible with Lévi-Strauss's idea of recurring cross-cultural structures.[2]

Lévi-Strauss's consideration of "magic" in chapter 9 reflects his engagement with the contemporary disciplines of psychology and physiology. "We [now] understand more clearly the psycho-physiological mechanisms underlying the instances reported from many parts of the world of death by exorcism and the casting of spells," he writes.[3] His analysis concentrates on the practice of people who are thought to have the power of healing, contrasting this briefly with Western* practices in psychotherapy. Here again he identifies systems of relationships between the people involved in healing in all cultures. He argues that all participants—the healer, the sick person, and the community—have separate and particular parts to play in a ritual performance.[4]

Overlooked

The essays collected in *Structural Anthropology* demonstrate Lévi-Strauss's consistent analytical use of binary oppositions throughout his career. Despite this, Lévi-Strauss ultimately rejected the idea of binary opposition as a determining principle in his discussion of social organization. He concluded that "the study of so-called dual organization discloses so many anomalies [unexplained results] ... that we should be well advised to reject the theory."[5] This rejection is due to the reality that social organization is ultimately too complex for the binary approach to be completely accurate.

A second topic of interest in *Structural Anthropology* that has escaped significant critical reflection has to do with Lévi-Strauss's interest in material culture—roughly, the physical things that help us to define a culture. He argued that comparative analysis of art in very different cultures allows the observer to appreciate similarities and trends that point to a universal psychology.[6] Lévi-Strauss notes that anthropologists had been reluctant to deal with comparisons of "primitive art."[7] He is not so reluctant, but unlike other anthropologists, who enjoyed fieldwork,* he chose to deal with art and material culture at a safe distance. This is revealed by the choice of photography and reproduced images in *Structural Anthropology*. The only photographs in the text appear in the chapter on art, and focus on pieces that were either from the author's collection or owned by museums, rather than showing them in their original context.

This sense of distance from "the field" is an important and repeated pattern in Lévi-Strauss's scholarly method and points to his main interest: the large-scale cross-cultural comparison that could not be performed by doing long-term fieldwork in one place (which was increasingly typical of anthropology). It was only this sense of perspective that enabled Lévi-Strauss to identify deep similarities among cultures.

NOTES

1   Claude Lévi-Strauss. *Structural Anthropology*, trans. Claire Jacobson and Brooke Grundfest Schoepf (New York: Basic Books, 1963), 3–5.

2   Claude Lévi-Strauss, *Totemism*, trans. R. Needham (Boston, MA: Beacon Press, 1963), 85.

3   Lévi-Strauss, *Structural Anthropology*, 167.

4   Lévi-Strauss, *Structural Anthropology*, 182.

5   Lévi-Strauss, *Structural Anthropology*, 161.

6   Lévi-Strauss, *Structural Anthropology*, 248.

7   Lévi-Strauss, *Structural Anthropology*, 245.

MODULE 7
ACHIEVEMENT

KEY POINTS

- *Structural Anthropology* successfully articulates Lévi-Strauss's view of the basic, underlying structure of human culture.*

- Lévi-Strauss helps elevate anthropology* to a scientific discipline in its own right.

- He begins an enduring conversation about how to describe and understand the human experience.

Assessing the Argument

In *Structural Anthropology*, Claude Lévi-Strauss presents a series of papers that develop a framework for analyzing human culture through the structures that define it. He outlines how we might use techniques derived from the field of linguistics* in the field of anthropology, focusing on the structures of kinship,* myth,* and symbolism.

Having originated in linguistics, the idea of structural analysis was not new. In *Structural Anthropology*, however, Lévi-Strauss uses this type of analysis in a new way, and with a new objective. He is interested in finding basic structures and relations that are common to many human cultures. He examines cultures separated from each other in both time and space in order to test for universal structures.

Lévi-Strauss makes use of ethnographic* data, both from his own limited period of fieldwork* and from others who had spent extended periods of time living and working among the world's premodern* peoples. Using practices similar to those of linguists, he proposes that invisible (and sometimes unconscious) structures support human culture; some critics, however, found this argument about "unconscious process" to be unconvincing.[1]

> **❝** The argument almost ceases to be comprehensible, yet even so ... the reader may suspect that behind the nonsense there is a sense. **❞**
>
> Edmund Leach, *Lévi-Strauss*

Using examples such as kinship and myth, Lévi-Strauss makes a case for structuralism* as a powerful theoretical lens for understanding human culture.

Achievement in Context

Lévi-Strauss's achievement in *Structural Anthropology* may be seen in terms of the extensive and long-lasting debate it stimulated. He was keen to separate anthropology from sociology,* and he helped to achieve this. His work was indebted to predecessors like the pioneering sociologists Émile Durkheim* and Marcel Mauss,* and to contemporaries like Roman Jakobson,* noted for his role in the development of structural linguistics.*

The work and life of Lévi-Strauss and his peers were affected greatly by the climate in France between World Wars I* and II.* In an intellectual vacuum, these scholars sought their own intellectual framework, finding that they largely rejected the viewpoints of their predecessors. World War II drove Lévi-Strauss and others into exile, again affecting and creating their intellectual viewpoints.

The publication of *Structural Anthropology* and the resulting criticism and related new schools of thought had important implications for the social sciences.* The search for answers about human culture occupied these social scientists, and Lévi-Strauss provided enormous food for thought. His search for cultural forms generated by unconscious structures was an attractive approach—it was appealing especially since it engaged topics like kinship, myth, and art. In the wake of a world war that had seen so much persecution and division, the implication of the structural approach—that peoples and cultures were more alike than they were different—was a new and welcome cultural assessment.

Limitations

Responses to Lévi-Strauss vary. Some praise the idea and the intellectualism of *Structural Anthropology* while simultaneously taking exception to its methods and conclusions, as well as to the way it handles evidence. In 1970, the British anthropologist Edmund Leach* observed that "despite … [Lévi-Strauss's] immense prestige, the critics among his profession greatly outnumber his disciples."[2]

This seems to be characteristic of responses to *Structural Anthropology*. Many who have engaged with the text have come away frustrated. Reactions tend to either praise its intellectual boldness from an overall point of view or to criticize from a closer perspective its lack of observable evidence, and repeated exclusion of case studies that challenge the arguments it makes. Most seriously, Lévi-Strauss's dislike of fieldwork and preference for large-scale comparative projects that used preexisting data was in conflict with the increasingly fieldwork-focused discipline of anthropology.

When Lévi-Strauss died in 2008, the world reacted in mixed ways to his intellectual career—most of these reactions seem superficial, perhaps because of a lack of engagement with the nature of his actual ideas. An obituary in the *Washington Post* quoted his disciple and successor Philippe Descola,* chairman of anthropology at the Collège de France,* who called Lévi-Strauss "one of the great intellectual heroes of the 20th century … He gave a proper object to anthropology: not simply as a study of human nature, but a systematic study of how cultural practices vary, how cultural differences are systematically organized."[3] Descola's praise is lavish, but the more general reaction seems to be that *Structural Anthropology* is a monumental, if flawed, work that is perhaps no longer relevant.

NOTES

1   J. R. Fox, "Review of *Structural Anthropology* by Claude Lévi-Strauss," *British Journal of Sociology* 16, no. 3 (September 1965), 268.

2   Edmund Leach, *Lévi-Strauss*, 1st edn (London: Fontana Press, 1970), 3.

3   Alexander F. Remington, "Renowned Anthropologist Claude Lévi-Strauss Dies at 100," *Washington Post,* November 5, 2009, accessed January 29, 2016, http://www.washingtonpost.com/wp-dyn/content/article/2009/11/03/AR2009110301477.html.

MODULE 8
PLACE IN THE AUTHOR'S WORK

KEY POINTS

- *Structural Anthropology* is the intellectual foundation of Claude Lévi-Strauss's entire career, which was devoted to answering the question "What is Man?"

- *Structural Anthropology* was strongly influenced by the extended periods during which Lévi-Strauss left his native France for Brazil and, later, the United States.

- Lévi-Strauss's *Tristes Tropiques* (*The Sad Tropics*) and *La Pensée sauvage* (*The Savage Mind*) are otherwise his most widely known works.

Positioning

Structural Anthropology as a whole represents a period of reflection in Claude Lévi-Strauss's intellectual career. Prior to joining a cultural mission to Brazil in 1935, his published output had been nonexistent. The mission to Brazil, and the fieldwork* associated with it, launched Lévi-Strauss on a new intellectual journey. His wartime exile in New York City proved a very productive time, and he benefitted from the community of American academics and of foreigners who had moved to the United States. It was in New York—by his own account—that he became an anthropologist.[1]*

Lévi-Strauss spent endless hours in the New York City Public Library, examining masses of ethnographic* data. During his time in New York, Lévi-Strauss produced his first major work, *Family and Social Life of the Nambikwara Indians,* which was published in Paris in 1948.[2] This was his first discussion of his ideas about kinship* studies and was presented as part of his doctoral thesis. In 1949 Lévi-Strauss

> **❝** Levi–Strauss' central intellectual puzzle is one to which European philosophers have returned over and over again; indeed if we accept Levi–Strauss' own view of the matter it is a problem which puzzles all mankind, everywhere, always. Quite simply: What is Man? **❞**
>
> Edmund Leach, *Lévi-Strauss*

continued his exploration with *The Elementary Structures of Kinship*.[3] In 1955 he published *Tristes Tropiques*, a somewhat autobiographical account of his fieldwork in Brazil, regarded by many critics as one of his most readable works.[4]

Integration

The main ideas in *Structural Anthropology* can be considered the intellectual and theoretical foundation of Lévi-Strauss's lifetime of scholarship. Throughout his work Lévi-Strauss searches for the answer to the eternal question of "What is Man?"[5] Lévi-Strauss developed his ideas about structuralism* during the 1940s and 1950s, and the papers collected to form *Structural Anthropology* represent the work of this period. *Structural Anthropology* appeared in 1958 in French, with the English translation following in 1963. Another key work appeared in 1962, *La Pensée sauvage* (later translated as *The Savage Mind*),[6] examining the workings of the "untamed" human mind. It was followed in 1962 by *Le Totémisme aujourd'hui* (later translated as *Totemism*), an important work on totems:* the use of plants or animals as symbols for families or cultural groups.[7] Lévi-Strauss published a second part of *Structural Anthropology* in 1973,[8] and continued to work and publish for the bulk of his lifetime, investigating structuralism while also thinking about totems, myth,* and methods for producing food.

Significance

Lévi-Strauss's work has proved to be significant and lasting. His career coincided with important intellectual movements—not only those shaping the discipline of anthropology,* but also those shaping bodies of thought centered on nationalist identities. Lévi-Strauss's own identity strongly influenced his own experience. As a French Jew, he endured forced exile from France, lest he suffer a worse fate as a result of Germany's Nazi* government, which killed millions of Jews. While exiled in New York, Lévi-Strauss developed his interest in the observation of universal elements of humankind. His own period of field observation in Brazil gave way to another kind of observation, that of the scholar. His body of work uses the principles of structuralism to explore how human societies function.

NOTES

1   Christopher Johnson, *Claude Lévi-Strauss: The Formative Years* (Cambridge: Cambridge University Press, 2003), 8–9.

2   Claude Lévi-Strauss, *La Vie familiale et sociale des indiens Nambikwara* (Paris: Au siège de la société, Musée de l'Homme, 1948).

3   Claude Lévi-Strauss, *Les Structures élémentaires de la parenté* (Paris: Presses universitaires de France, 1949).

4   Susan Sontag, *Against Interpretation: And Other Essays* (New York: Farrar, Straus and Giroux, 1966).

5   Edmund Leach, *Lévi-Strauss*, 4th edn (London: Fontana Press, 1996), 47.

6   Claude Lévi-Strauss, *La Pensée sauvage* (Paris: Plon, 1962).

7   Claude Lévi-Strauss, *Le Totémisme aujourd'hui* (Paris: Presses universitaires de France, 1962). The English edition was *Totemism*, tran. R. Needham (Boston, MA: Beacon Press, 1963).

8   Claude Lévi-Strauss, *Anthropologie structurale deux* (Paris: Plon, 1973). Biafran Civil War* of the late 1960s. Achebe's outstanding reputation as a thinker and expert in postcolonial criticism remains to the present day.

SECTION 3
IMPACT

MODULE 9
THE FIRST RESPONSES

KEY POINTS

- *Structural Anthropology* attracted a great deal of scholarly commentary, both positive and negative.

- While Claude Lévi-Strauss was praised for expanding the horizons of anthropology, some of his specific ideas drew harsh criticism, as did some of his research methods.

- Although *Structural Anthropology* made important contributions to expanding and reshaping the discipline of anthropology, his ideas about the universal nature of cultures* are not universally accepted.

Criticism

If we judge Claude Lévi-Strauss's *Structural Anthropology* on the basis of the quantity and passion of critical responses, then the work must be considered quite successful. In the decades after the book's publication, virtually every aspect of the work was assessed critically. Some critics were harsh, seeing the work as a sort of intellectual "cult" practicing a vaguely defined method of psychological* oversimplification.[1]

During the 1960s there were various close readings, especially by scholars such as the political philosopher Louis Althusser,* the literary theorist Roland Barthes,* the philosopher and intellectual historian Michel Foucault,* and the psychoanalyst* Jacques Lacan.* These scholars continued the examination of structuralism* launched by Lévi-Strauss, all while rejecting parts of his work. Barthes felt that the language-like pattern that Lévi-Strauss considered universal was in fact quite subjective,* meaning it was based on Lévi-Strauss's opinion rather than on fact. Like Barthes, Lacan also challenged the idea of

> ❝ In France, where there is more awareness of the adventure, the *risk* involved in intelligence, a man can be both a specialist and the subject of general and intelligent interest and controversy. ❞
>
> Susan Sontag, "A Hero of our Time," *New York Review of Books*

universality in culture. Others pointed out shortcomings in Lévi-Strauss's evidence-gathering. So while Lévi-Strauss's work was praised in general for expanding the field of anthropology,* it was widely criticized for various, more specific reasons.

Responses

In the *American Journal of Sociology,* the anthropologist Charles Ackerman* praised *Structural Anthropology* by discussing its relevance to action theory, a branch of philosophy* examining how physical behavior is influenced by a person's beliefs and desires. According to Ackerman, "Claude Lévi-Strauss's 'structure' may seem to many an alien and strange thing; to action-theorists it will not. Action-theorists interested in primitive societies must welcome *Structural Anthropology* as one of the rare great works of contemporary social-anthropological analysis. Brilliantly inexact, Lévi-Strauss has transfigured inexactitude; a vice of many, it is one of his virtues—a technique."[2]

However, some critics have identified severe limitations in the theory itself, such as a failure to engage fully with existentialism.* This is a form of philosophy that emphasizes individuals' freedom, and ability to affect their lives through the choices they make, and it was influential among Lévi-Strauss's French intellectual peers.

In terms of formal recognition, the world of academia responded with approval to Lévi-Strauss and his work. One year after the French publication of *Anthropologie structurale*, Lévi-Strauss became chair of anthropology in the Collège de France,* a research institution founded nearly five centuries ago in Paris; he held the post until 1982. Among other honors, in 1973 Lévi-Strauss received the Erasmus Prize,* which is awarded for notable contributions to European culture, society, or social science.

Conflict and Consensus

Some anthropologists today consider Lévi-Strauss's work on structuralism to be important for historical reasons, but largely outdated.[3] The original work is both complex and entangled, as is its later tradition of criticism, reaction, and evaluation. One interesting intellectual overlap was the reception of structuralism among Marxist* philosophers (those philosophers influenced by the social and historical analysis of the nineteenth-century political philosopher Karl Marx).* Although many Marxists found structuralism wanting, there was considerable overlap between the two because of Marxism's emphasis on the power of structures.[4] Indeed, the French Marxist philosopher Louis Althusser formed a perspective called "Structural Marxism."

Among anthropologists, critics found that Lévi-Strauss's approach in *Structural Anthropology* relied largely on the idea that primitive people were somehow purer than Western* cultures, and that the theory lacked both historical and individual support. In short, the work was seen as lacking scientific objectivity,* meaning it was considered to be based more on Lévi-Strauss's personal opinions than on observed fact.

Lévi-Strauss responded to these criticisms in several ways, in part by saying his work had been misunderstood. His responses to his critics were not very strong or effective. One notable response came in the form of a change of focus in his later work, perhaps an unconscious reaction to the critics. In his continuing, formal work, his methods changed, and the universalism that was so central to *Structural Anthropology* largely went away. In his text *La Pensée sauvage* (*The Savage*

Mind),[5] Lévi-Strauss explored the workings of the human brain in ways that differed from *Structural Anthropology,* focusing instead on how the unconscious mind is expressed in physical behavior. In his work on mythology,*[6] Lévi-Strauss explored "myth cycles" (large, associated bodies of myth) but largely avoided kinship* analysis.

NOTES

1   J. R. Fox, "Review of *Structural Anthropology* by Claude Lévi-Strauss," *British Journal of Sociology* 16, no. 3 (September 1965): 268.

2   Charles Ackerman, "Review of *Structural Anthropology* by Claude Lévi-Strauss," *American Journal of Sociology* 71, no. 2 (September 1965): 215.

3   André-Georges Hardricourt and Georges Granai, "Linguistique et sociologie," *Cahiers internationaux de Sociologie* 19, 2nd series (1955): 114–29; Maxime Rodinson, "Ethnographie et relativisme," *La Nouvelle Critique* 69 (1955): 49–63.

4   Terry Eagleton, *Literary Theory: An Introduction* (Oxford: Blackwell, 1983), 109.

5   See Claude Lévi-Strauss, *The Savage Mind* (Chicago: University of Chicago Press, 1966).

6   See Claude Lévi-Strauss, *The Raw and the Cooked,* vol. 1 of *Mythologiques,* trans. John Weightman and Doreen Weightman (New York: Harper & Row, 1969); Claude Lévi-Strauss, *From Honey to Ashes*, vol. 2 of *Mythologiques,* trans. John Weightman and Doreen Weightman (New York: Harper & Row, 1973); Claude Lévi-Strauss, *The Origin of Table Manners*, vol. 3 of *Mythologiques,* trans. John Weightman and Doreen Weightman (New York: Harper & Row, 1978); Claude Lévi-Strauss, *The Naked Man,* vol. 4 of *Mythologiques,* trans. John Weightman and Doreen Weightman (New York: Harper & Row, 1981).

THE EVOLVING DEBATE

KEY POINTS

- The debate on structuralism* continues in the discipline of anthropology.*

- *Structural Anthropology* and its focus on structuralism gave birth to opposing movements, including poststructuralism.*

- Beyond anthropology, structuralism has been important to the development of archaeological* theory.

Uses and Problems

Claude Lévi-Strauss published *Structural Anthropology* nearly 60 years ago. The book still stands as a monument to anthropological theory and as a platform for continuing debate among anthropologists who seek to understand human culture.* The American anthropologist Marshall Sahlins,* writing in Lévi-Strauss's 100th year, acknowledged how deeply ingrained Lévi-Strauss's ideas have been within the discipline of anthropology. For Sahlins, "Many anthropologists who would not identify themselves as structuralists—including many who condemn and shun the 's-word'—have nevertheless been inspired by one or another aspect or implication of his work."[1] Sahlins sees that work as continuing.

Some responses to *Structural Anthropology* accused Lévi-Strauss of lacking objectivity.* His attempts to explain structuralism involved the use of evidence that could not be independently verified and did not consider cases that appeared to challenge his ideas. This was perhaps in part because of Lévi-Strauss's relative lack of experience in fieldwork* (firsthand data-gathering), which could have provided a more varied range of cases.[2] However, even if his theory had flawed

> ❝ The writings of Lévi-Strauss have left a broad wake of effervescent admirers and roiled specialists. Not many have attempted to check the evidence he advances in support of a thesis or have tried to verify his findings. Those who have closely examined specific writings have generally found them deficient in both respects. ❞
>
> David Mandelbaum, "Myths and Myth Maker," *Ethnology*

evidence, later anthropologists were able to investigate his ideas as a theoretical approach during fieldwork. This showed the ongoing exchange between theory and method in anthropology.

Schools of Thought

Structuralism gave birth in short order to poststructuralism. It is often difficult to tell the difference between these two closely related intellectual movements. Poststructuralism in the humanities* and social sciences* involved an increased focus on historical method, and challenged the assumption that objective analysis was possible. This turn to an emphasis on the subjective* (according to which individual judgment is shaped by personal history, circumstances and opinion, rather than by objective "truths") was made in order to demonstrate the limits of structuralism, which had claimed a level of objectivity by avoiding discussion of subjective factors in analytical method. Meanwhile, in development studies, a political neostructuralism* has emerged in recent years, arguing that governments must play an active role in order to improve a society's economic and social welfare.[3]

In poststructural British anthropology, Rodney Needham* and Edmund Leach* both draw influence from the work of Lévi-Strauss, although they do not embrace his work entirely. Leach examines "real life" from a structural point of view, rather than searching for universal structures.[4] While he sees value in Lévi-Strauss's framework, he calls for more data and more probing analysis. For him, Lévi-Strauss is too distant from the actual data that could prove his argument.

In his *History of Structuralism*, the historian François Dosse* said in the 1990s that structuralism and its offshoots remain intellectually important in spite of repeated challenges.[5]

In Current Scholarship

One of the key applications of structuralism today in the social sciences is in the field of archaeology,* the study of past human culture through recovered material items such as buildings, roads, art, and housewares. It is likely that Lévi-Strauss would have appreciated this application of his ideas, given his early interest in geology, as well as his chapter in *Structural Anthropology* on art. Around the same time that Lévi-Strauss was set to publish the 1958 French edition of *Structural Anthropology*, the archaeologists Gordon Willey* and Philip Phillips* declared that "American archaeology is anthropology or it is nothing."[6] This was the beginning of processual archaeology.*

Processualists suggested that by rigorously applying scientific method,* archaeologists could understand the historical processes that caused change to happen in the past.[7] Those who advocated this new approach saw a parallel between anthropological method, which observed living humans, and archaeology, which examined the material remains of the human past.

Eventually, as with all theoretical schools, a counter approach developed—postprocessual* or interpretive archaeology. This school reacts against processualism as some critics reacted against structuralism, arguing that archaeological interpretation is necessarily subjective, and thus that the interpretation says as much about the observer as it does about the observed (or more so).[8]

NOTES

1   Marshall Sahlins, "On the Anthropology of Levi-Strauss," American Anthropological Association blog, July 7, 2009, accessed February 2, 2016, http://blog.americananthro.org/2009/07/07/on-the-anthropology-of-levi-strauss/.

2   Pascal Boyer, "Explaining Religious Concepts: Lévi-Strauss the Brilliant and Problematic Ancestor," in *Mental Culture, Classical Social Theory and the Cognitive Science of Religion*, ed. Dimitris Xygalatas and Lee McCorkle (Durham: Acumen): 164–75.

3   World Economics Association, "Interview on Neo-structuralism," World Economics Association website, accessed February 2, 2016, http://www.worldeconomicsassociation.org/newsletterarticles/neo-structuralism/.

4   Edmund Leach, *Political Systems of Highland Burma* (London: Bell, 1954).

5   François Dosse, *The Sign Sets: 1967—Present, vol. 2 of History of Structuralism*, trans. Deborah Glassman (Minneapolis, MN: University of Minnesota Press, 1997).

6   Gordon Willey and Philip Phillips, *Method and Theory in American Archaeology* (Chicago: University of Chicago Press, 1958).

7   Bruce Trigger, *A History of Archaeological Thought* (New York: Cambridge University Press, 1989): 148.

8   Ian Hodder, ed., *Symbolic and Structural Archaeology* (Cambridge: Cambridge University Press, 1982).

IMPACT AND INFLUENCE TODAY

KEY POINTS

- *Structural Anthropology* and the work of Claude Lévi-Strauss remain significant to the "conversation" in the social sciences.*

- Poststructural* theory builds upon structuralism* and takes up often contrary viewpoints.

- The deconstruction* movement, which focuses on the meaning of words in relation to each other, arose in part as a challenge to structuralism.

Position

As one of the greatest anthropologists of the twentieth century, Claude Lévi-Strauss and his writing, including *Structural Anthropology*, still occupies a prominent place in the intellectual history of the social sciences. His body of work is massive, the abundant output of a mind constantly in action—his work on myth,* for example, spans four volumes.[1]

In her review of a biography of Lévi-Strauss published in 2000,[2] professor Michèle Richman* sees him as scientifically relevant in the late twentieth century, but says he is simultaneously being "eclipsed within his own society."[3] Perhaps this is a result of being a perpetual outsider, as observed by the American cultural critic Susan Sontag:* "The anthropologist's vocation requires the assumption of a profound detachment. Never can he feel himself 'at home' anywhere; he will always be, psychologically, an amputee."[4]

We must not forget, either, that Lévi-Strauss was a very private person, disliking public occasions and self-publicity as he became increasingly elderly.[5]

> **❝** Among the most renowned of contemporary studies of myth are the works of Claude Lévi-Strauss. A prolific author, vastly erudite and industrious, he is one of the most discussed thinkers of his time in literary, linguistic, anthropological, philosophic, and even some political circles. **❞**
>
> David Mandelbaum, "Myths and Myth Maker," *Ethnology*

In 1967, the French philosopher Jacques Derrida* published *Of Grammatology*, giving expression to a form of poststructural thought that launched the deconstruction movement,[6] which focuses on the internal workings and assumptions of language. In an influential lecture delivered in the United States at Johns Hopkins University the previous year, Derrida had focused on the theoretical limitations of structuralism, drawing on Lévi-Strauss's work.[7]

Derrida argued that binary oppositions* "play" with each other: one term always refers to another (for example "being" can only be understood in opposition to "nothing"), and so they exist only in relation to one another. This means that there is no foundational meaning that lies underneath this process. Derrida argued that structuralism, despite relying on dynamic binary oppositions, still assumed that there was a foundational "anchoring" structure or meaning underneath the binary process. Derrida argued that this did not exist, and that it would be more scientific to deconstruct further the relationship between binary oppositions, and come up with new terms.

Interestingly, Lévi-Strauss himself had noted the imperfection of the binary structure, perhaps paving the way for more analysis of relationships between terms.[8] Today deconstruction remains an important approach in art, architecture, and literary criticism.

Interaction

Structural Anthropology remains relevant within the social sciences. It continues to be standard reading for post-secondary and professional students in anthropology* and sociology.* There is still something of an intellectual cult attached to Lévi-Strauss and his work. A variety of handbooks focused on the man and on his body of work continue to appear; Edmund Leach's* well-known commentary on Lévi-Strauss's key ideas has seen four editions issued.[9]

Lévi-Strauss's work has influenced specialists in other fields of social science as well and has sparked its fair share of debate about the approach, methods, and conclusions reached. The American anthropologist David Mandelbaum* describes how Lévi-Strauss's work in *Structural Anthropology* has influenced other anthropologists who wanted to conduct their own structural analyses.

He notes that "some research workers have built structuralist analyses on the basis of observed behavior and have returned to the observational base in order to test the validity of the formulations as they may be manifest in people's lives."[10] This is an important observation. It notices that Lévi-Strauss's work stresses observation in order to discover structural elements. It also notices that in applying structuralism some social scientists see the need to consider alternative explanations in a way that is sometimes absent in Lévi-Strauss's writings.

Increased attention to the subjectivity* of the anthropologist has also been productive, as the relationship between the observer and the observed is an important consideration when trying to reach universal conclusions about humankind.

The Continuing Debate

In the 1960s and 1970s the reactions to structuralism included the emergence of poststructuralism. This framework of thinking emerged as a result of debates within the social sciences and humanities.*

Poststructuralists, including the French scholars Jacques Derrida, Michel Foucault,* and Jacques Lacan,* tend to reject Lévi-Strauss's idea that elements of human culture* are linked by universal structures.[11]

Roland Barthes,* a French literary scholar, argued that the structural patterns that Lévi-Strauss describes as universal are in fact limited by Lévi-Strauss's own "Westernized"* frame of reference. Lacan objected to the idea of universality. He felt that Lévi-Strauss's focus on the "unconscious activity of the mind"[12] resulted in the removal of any objectivity* (impartial observation). These reactions in the decades after the publication of *Structural Anthropology* tend to be divided along lines of nationalism and language.

NOTES

1   Claude Lévi-Strauss, *Mythologiques*, vols. 1–4, trans. John Weightman and Doreen Weightman (Paris: Plon, 1964–71).

2   Marcel Hénaff, *Claude Lévi-Strauss and the Making of Structural Anthropology*, trans. Mary Baker (Minnesota: University of Minnesota Press, 1998).

3   Michèle Richman, "Review of *Claude Lévi-Strauss and the Making of Structural Anthropology* by Marcel Hénaff," *SubStance* 29, no. 3 issue 93: special issue: Pierre Bourdieu (2000): 132–4.

4   Susan Sontag, *Against Interpretation: And Other Essays*, (New York: Farrar, Straus and Giroux, 1966), 74.

5   Maurice Bloch, "Claude Lévi-Strauss Obituary," *Guardian*, November 3, 2009, accessed February 2, 2016, http://www.theguardian.com/science/2009/nov/03/claude-levi-strauss-obituary.

6   Jacques Derrida, *Of Grammatology*, trans. Gayatri Chakravorty Spivak (Baltimore: Johns Hopkins University, 1976).

7   Derrida delivered the lecture "Structure, Sign, and Play in the Discourse of the Human Sciences" on October 21, 1966, and published it as a chapter of *Writing and Difference* in 1967.

MODULE 12
WHERE NEXT?

KEY POINTS

- It is likely that *Structural Anthropology* will continue to be a foundational work of anthropology.*
- Increasing globalization* is eroding the differences between cultures,* as Claude Lévi-Strauss predicted.
- Structuralism* continues to be an important tool in the field of archaeology.*

Potential

It seems quite likely that Claude Lévi-Strauss's *Structural Anthropology* will continue to be a key work for the discipline of anthropology. More than 50 years have passed since its first publication, and structuralism continues to be taught in university departments and to generate debate. On Lévi-Strauss's death at the age of 100, his work was declared dead by some literary critics, who said this judgment had been delayed as a mark of respect for an elderly man.[1]

Despite this, and despite earlier declarations that structuralism was a thing of the past, the approach seems to have enough influence to carry it forward to new generations of thinkers, even if they ultimately choose to leave Lévi-Strauss's own ideas about structuralism behind. It is also worth noting that the opinions of Lévi-Strauss's work in France often differ from the world beyond. English-speaking scholars and students were slower to study all the elements of Lévi-Strauss's work. As a result, structuralism is more influential in English-language studies of anthropology, at the very least as a critical part of the discipline's intellectual history.

> ❝ Finding one's way through this potent stuff was wonderful and wonderfully confusing. I doubt there has been an intellectual and emotional revolution of this profundity since the advent of the 'historical avant-garde' in the early twentieth century. ❞
>
> Michael Taussig, "Call to Order" *Artforum International*

Future Directions

Our world is growing smaller. Claude Lévi-Strauss disliked the dominance of European thought and culture, concerned that non-European "primitive" societies would be absorbed and erased. In the globalizing environment of today's world, Lévi-Strauss's concern seems like a good prediction. Globalization—the tendency of the world's cultures to grow ever closer together by means of economic and technological convergence—is an important topic for social scientists today. It seems certain that globalization will continue to have a homogenizing* effect—moving toward a sameness—that reduces the benefits of having multiple traditions and eats away at less powerful cultures.

In archaeology, a field related to that of anthropology, structuralism continues to provide a framework for research. Archaeological theorists see it as a tool for insight and inquiry. Structuralism contributed to postprocessual* theory in archaeology, which holds that any archaeological interpretation necessarily depends on the opinions and background of the observer. Even now, more than 25 years after the beginnings of the postprocessualism movement, archaeologists acknowledge a need for structuralism in archaeology. It provides a systematic tool for assessing the "reconstructions of meanings from past cultures."[2] As the postprocessual movement continues even now, theoretical practitioners see an almost endless usefulness for structuralism, as it offers an ever-expanding means of understanding human culture and behavior.[3]

Summary

Structural Anthropology was initially an obscure work from a French thinker whose forced exile from France gave him a different experience from that of a Frenchman living in France. As the book gained wider exposure along with Lévi-Strauss's other work, it became clear that *Structural Anthropology* had made an important contribution to the social sciences.*

As an exiled Frenchman experiencing the world as an outsider, Lévi-Strauss borrowed from structural linguistics* to search for the most essential elements of human culture. By applying his structuralist thinking to various aspects of culture—kinship,* myth,* ritual, art— Lévi-Strauss demonstrated creative thinking, even if some anthropologists took exception to his specific methods.

Most students encounter Lévi-Strauss as a giant of anthropology whose philosophical and sometimes vague prose does not seem to provide a clear way to understand the human condition. But perhaps Lévi-Strauss is best understood as a somewhat romantic philosopher who sought the key to the human condition and mourned the loss of cultural differences at the hands of Western* society. For these reasons, and others, *Structural Anthropology* is still considered a "must-read" in the field, even though many of his specific theories are widely rejected.

NOTES

1   Vincent Debane, "Lévi-Strauss, homme des lettres," in *Claude Lévi-Strauss: l'homme derrière l'oeuvre*, ed. Émilie Joulia (Paris: Lattès, 2008), 27.

2   R. Layton, "Structuralism and Semiotics," in *Handbook of Material Culture*, ed. Christopher Tilley et al. (London: Sage, 2006): 29–42.

3   "Structural Archaeology," in Claire Smith, ed., *Encyclopedia of Global Archaeology* (New York: Springer-Verlag, 2014).

GLOSSARY

GLOSSARY OF TERMS

Académie Française: a prestigious council established in France in 1635 that determines official recommendations regarding use of the French language.

Agency: the capacity of individuals to act effectively under certain conditions.

Agrégation: a competitive civil service examination for some positions in the public education system in France.

Anthropology: the study of human social and cultural life, including domains "at home" as well as those of distant countries.

Archaeology: the study of past human social and cultural life through the excavation of material culture in its original setting. This includes buildings, roads, and art.

Binary opposition: a pair of concepts that gain their meaning from their opposition to each other—for example, hot/cold, raw/cooked, light/dark.

Bororo: an indigenous people of Brazil, living in the western state of Mato Grosso.

Collège de France: a prestigious higher education and research university in Paris, France.

Cultural institution (or social institution): a custom or convention that encapsulates, and helps maintain, the norms of the broader society and culture.

Cultural relativism: an analytical position that holds specific beliefs or behaviors are best understood in terms of their function within their culture, and should not be judged according to the world view or moral standards of the external onlooker.

Culture: the beliefs, traditions, social behaviors, and artistic or literary expression of a particular group of people.

Deconstruction: a poststructuralist literary approach concerned with meaning and proposed by Jacques Derrida. It analyzes the relationships both between signs and between binary oppositions.

École Pratique des Hautes Études: one of France's most prestigious research and higher education institutions.

Empiricism: a theory that all knowledge is derived from sense experience.

Erasmus Prize: a prize awarded by the Praemium Erasmianum Foundation, a Dutch cultural institution, for exceptional contributions to culture, society, or social science.

Ethnography: the written text containing the findings and analysis of anthropological study; the practice of recording and collating such findings.

Ethnology: an old-fashioned term describing a branch of anthropology that took the data compiled by ethnographers and made cross-cultural comparisons.

Evolution: the process by which organisms improve themselves through progressive inherited change over time.

Existentialism: a form of philosophy that emphasizes individuals' existence, freedom, and ability to affect their lives through the choices they make.

Fieldwork: in regard to anthropology, the practice of conducting social scientific investigation among human societies, usually for extended periods of time.

Globalization: the process of connection through the increased international circulation of ideas, products, and persons.

Guaycuru: several separate but related ethnic groups, indigenous to the Gran Chaco area in South America.

Holocaust: the persecution and murder of millions of European Jews and other minorities by the German Nazi regime, 1933–45.

Homogenization: the process of making entities similar that were previously unlike one another, usually by one entity's features surviving those of the other.

Humanities: academic disciplines that study human culture, including politics, history, and literature.

Indigenous: with regard to people, those who claim original historical ties to a particular land or nation.

Kinship: the network of social relationships that form an important part of the lives of most human societies.

Kinship terms: terminologies used by a group to define familial relationships.

Linguistics: the scientific and social scientific study of language.

Marxism: a philosophical, political, and economic form of socialism, derived from the work of the political philosopher Karl Marx, holding that class struggle will only end when society inevitably moves from oppression by elites to a classless social order.

Myth: a traditional story, especially one that concerns the early history of a people or explains natural phenomena. Myth typically involves supernatural beings or events.

Nambikwara: (also called Nambikuára) an indigenous people of Brazil, living in the Amazon.

Nazi: extreme right-wing political party that ruled Germany between 1933 and 1945. The Nazis (short for National Socialists) were led by Adolf Hitler.

Neostructuralism: a movement in development studies advocating the increased role of the state in the economic and social welfare of its people.

New School for Social Research: a progressive university in New York City, founded in 1919.

Objectivity: a lack of bias or prejudice.

Oedipus: a mythical Greek king of Thebes known best from the tragedies of the ancient Greek playwright Sophocles.

Philosophy: the study of the universal nature of reality, knowledge, values, and reason.

Phoneme: any of the distinct units of sound in a specified language that distinguish one word from another.

Physiology: the study of the normal functions of living things.

Postprocessual archaeology: a theoretical school that emphasizes the inherent subjectivity of archaeological interpretations.

Poststructural: a late twentieth-century philosophy that opposes the popular structuralist movement that preceded it in France during the 1950s and 1960s.

Premodern: anticipating the modern phase or period of something while not actually belonging to it. In terms of culture, formerly referred to as "primitive."

Processual archaeology: approach in archaeology that argues the rigorous application of the scientific method can yield information about a culture. This application studies the process of human activities and the means by which things decay or degrade.

Psychoanalysis: a therapeutic and theoretical approach to the unconscious mind developed in the late nineteenth and early twentieth centuries by the Austrian neurologist Sigmund Freud.

Psychology: the study of the human mind and behavior.

Scientific method: a way of systematically constructing knowledge, through the repeated relationship between observation, hypothesis (an explanation for a phenomenon made on the basis of the available evidence), and investigation, which leads to further observation and so on.

Semiotics: the study of how meaning is made and communicated, often through signs.

Social facts: a term invented by the sociologist Émile Durkheim to describe cultural norms and social structures that exercised influence and power above and beyond the agency of the individual.

Social sciences: the academic disciplines that study the social life of human groups and individuals using scientific methods. They include anthropology, economics, geography, psychology, and sociology.

Sociology: the scientific study of social behavior, its origins, development, organization, and institutions.

Structuralism: in regards to anthropology, a theoretical position that holds that all cultures have certain organizing principles in common, and that cultures must be understood in their relation to these universal structures.

Structural linguistics: the study of language as a structure in which the meaning of every element is affected by its relationship to other parts of the language.

Subjectivity: the way in which individual judgment is shaped by personal history, circumstances, and opinion, rather than by objective "truths."

Totemism: the cultural belief that a social group has a spiritual connection with a particular animal or plant ("totem").

Tupi-Kawahib: an indigenous population of the Brazilian coast.

Université Paris-Sorbonne (Paris IV): a public research university in Paris, France.

Vichy government: the pro-Axis (Germany, Italy and Japan) government of France headed by Marshal Philippe Pétain from 1940 to 1944 during World War II.

Western culture: a phrase used broadly to refer to European and American civilization, values, lifestyles, and arts.

World War I (1914–18): a global conflict triggered by the assassination of Archduke Franz Ferdinand in Sarajevo, Bosnia, and including considerable land, air, and sea fighting in Europe.

World War II (1939–45): a global conflict triggered by Adolf Hitler's invasion of Poland, and including the Holocaust of European Jews and the detonation of nuclear weapons in Japan.

PEOPLE MENTIONED IN THE TEXT

Charles Ackerman was a professor of anthropology at Cornell University in the 1960s.

Louis Althusser (1918–90) was a French Marxist philosopher and author of the influential volume *Reading Capital* (1965).

Roland Barthes (1915–80) was a French literary theorist interested in semiotics (the study of the way in which meaning is communicated through signs). He wrote *La Mort de l'auteur* (*The Death of the Author*), a key 1967 essay.

Simone de Beauvoir (1908–86) was a French philosopher and writer, known for writing *The Second Sex* (1949).

Franz Boas (1858–1942) was a German American anthropologist and is considered the "father" of American anthropology.

Lewis Carroll (1832–98), pen name of English writer and mathematician Charles Lutwidge Dodgson, author of *Alice's Adventures in Wonderland* (1865) and its sequel *Through the Looking-Glass, and What Alice Found There* (1871).

Jacques Derrida (1930–2004) was an Algerian-born French philosopher who advanced deconstruction, a form of semiotic analysis.

Philippe Descola (b. 1949) is a renowned French anthropologist who was a student of Claude Lévi-Strauss. His research focuses on the Achuar, a Jivaroan people in the Amazon basin in South America.

François Dosse (b. 1950) is a French historian particularly interested in cultural and intellectual history.

Émile Durkheim (1858–1917) was a French sociologist and philosopher who is regarded as one of the primary architects of modern social sciences and sociology.

Michel Foucault (1926–84) was a French philosopher and historian of ideas who explored the relationship between power and knowledge.

Sigmund Freud (1856–1939) was an Austrian neurologist who pioneered the field of psychoanalysis. He analyzed dreams and feelings to arrive at a wide-ranging critical assessment of culture and religion.

Roman Jakobson (1896–1982) was a linguist and literary theorist, known for *The Framework of Language* (1980).

Immanuel Kant (1724–1804) was a German philosopher who is renowned for his contributions across the discipline.

Julia Kristeva (b. 1941) is a Bulgarian French philosopher and literary critic.

Jacques Lacan (1901–81) was a French psychoanalyst and psychiatrist whose ideas influenced critical theory and literary theory.

Edmund Leach (1910–89) was a renowned British social anthropologist. He was provost of King's College, Cambridge, 1966–79.

Robert Lowie (1883–1957) was an Austrian-born American anthropologist and an expert on North American indigenous peoples.

Bronisław Malinowski (1884–1942) was an influential Polish anthropologist known for his ethnographic work among the Trobriand islanders (inhabitants of a group of coral atolls off the east coast of New Guinea).

David Mandelbaum (1911–87) was an American anthropologist whose research focused on First Nations peoples in Canada, and the structure of society in India.

Karl Marx (1818–83) was a German philosopher and socialist. His theories about class struggle and the best conditions for a flourishing society became known as Marxism.

Marcel Mauss (1872–1950) was a French sociologist whose 1925 work, *The Gift*, contributed to the emergence of anthropology as a separate discipline.

Rodney Needham (1923–2006) was an influential British anthropologist and structuralist who conducted fieldwork in Borneo and Malaysia.

Philip Phillips (1900–94) was an American archaeologist who studied the Mississippian culture of the Lower Mississippi Valley.

Michèle H. Richman is a professor of Romance languages at the University of Pennsylvania and studies the relations between literature, anthropology, and social criticism, especially in the twentieth century.

Alfred Radcliffe-Brown (1881–1955) was a British social anthropologist who pioneered the theory of coadaptation and structural functionalism.

Marshall Sahlins (b. 1930) is an American anthropologist best known for conducting ethnographic work in the Pacific, particularly Fiji and Hawaii.

Jean-Paul Sartre (1905–80) was a French philosopher, best known for his existentialist philosophy, which states an individual's experience of the world begins from a place of disorientation and confusion.

Ferdinand de Saussure (1857–1913) was a Swiss linguist who specialized in semiotics, or meaning-making within language. His work had a profound influence upon Lévi-Strauss.

Susan Sontag (1933–2004) was an American writer, cultural commentator, and activist. She is known particularly for her essays on photography and AIDS.

Gordon Willey (1913–2002) was an American archaeologist who earned his PhD at Columbia University. The so-called "dean" of New World archaeology,

WORKS CITED

WORKS CITED

Académie Française. "Claude Lévi-Strauss." Accessed November 1, 2015. http://www.academie-francaise.fr/les-immortels/claude-levi-strauss.

Ackerman, Charles. "Review of *Structural Anthropology* by Claude Lévi-Strauss." *American Journal of Sociology* 71, no. 2 (September 1965): 215.

Bloch, Maurice. "Claude Lévi-Strauss Obituary." *Guardian*, November 3, 2009. Accessed February 2, 2016. http://www.theguardian.com/science/2009/nov/03/claude-levi-strauss-obituary.

Boyer, Pascal. "Explaining Religious Concepts: Lévi-Strauss the Brilliant and Problematic Ancestor." In *Mental Culture, Classical Social Theory and the Cognitive Science of Religion*, edited by Dimitris Xygalatas and Lee McCorkle, 164–75. Durham: Acumen, 2013.

Carrère-d'Encausse, Hélène. "Adresse à M. le professeur Claude Lévi-Strauss à l'occasion de son centième anniversaire." Accessed November 1, 2015. http://www.academie-francaise.fr/adresse-m-le-professeur-claude-levi-strauss-loccasion-de-son-centieme-anniversaire.

Clarke, Simon. *The Foundations of Structuralism: A Critique of Lévi-Strauss and the Structuralist Movement*. Brighton, Sussex: Harvester Press; Totowa, N.J.: Barnes & Noble, 1981.

Crosby, Robert. "Structuralism and Lévi-Strauss." *The Harvard Crimson*, November 17, 1970. Accessed September 5, 2015. http://www.thecrimson.com/article/1970/11/17/structuralism-and-levi-strauss-pin-the-last/.

Debane, Vincent. "Lévi-Strauss, homme des lettres." In *Claude Lévi-Strauss: l'homme derrière l'oeuvre*, edited by Émilie Joulia, 27–41. Paris: Lattès, 2008.

Derrida, Jacques. *Of Grammatology.* Translated by Gayatri Chakravorty Spivak. Baltimore: Johns Hopkins University, 1976.

"Structure, Sign, and Play in the Discourse of the Human Sciences." In *Writing and Difference*, by Jacques Derrida, 278–94. Translated by Alan Bass. London: Routledge, 2001.

Dosse, François. *The Sign Sets: 1967—Present.* Vol. 2 of *History of Structuralism*. Translated by Deborah Glassman. Minneapolis, MN: University of Minnesota Press, 1997.

Durkheim, David Émile. *The Division of Labor in Society.* Translated by Lewis A. Coser. New York: The Free Press, 1984.

Eagleton, Terry. *Literary Theory: An Introduction*. Oxford: Blackwell, 1983.

Fox, J. R. "Review of *Structural Anthropology* by Claude Lévi-Strauss." *British Journal of Sociology* 16, no. 3 (September 1965): 268.

Hardricourt, André-Georges, and Georges Granai. "Linguistique et sociologie." *Cahiers Internationaux de Sociologie* 19, 2nd series (1955): 114–29.

Harrison, Paul. "Post-structural Theories." In *Approaches to Human Geography*, edited by S. Aitken and G. Valentine, 122–35. London: Sage, 2006.

Hénaff, Marcel. *Claude Lévi-Strauss and the Making of Structural Anthropology*. Translated by Mary Baker. Minnesota: University of Minnesota Press, 1998.

Hodder, Ian, ed. *Symbolic and Structural Archaeology*. Cambridge: Cambridge University Press, 1982.

Hughes, Henry Stuart. *The Obstructed Path: French Social Thought in the Years of Desperation, 1930–1960*. New Jersey: Harper & Row, 1968.

Johnson, Christopher. *Claude Lévi-Strauss: The Formative Years*. Cambridge: Cambridge University Press, 2003.

Kant, Immanuel. *Anthropology from a Pragmatic Point of View*. Translated by V. L. Dodwell and H. H. Rudnick. Carbondale, IL: Southern Illinois University Press, 1978.

Layton, R. "Structuralism and Semiotics." In *Handbook of Material Culture*, edited by Christopher Tilley, Webb Keane, Susanne Küchler, Mike Rowlands, and Patricia Speyer, 29–42. London: Sage, 2006.

Leach, Edmund. *Lévi-Strauss*, 1st edn. London: Fontana Press, 1970.

Lévi-Strauss, 4th edn. London: Fontana Press, 1996.

Political Systems of Highland Burma. London: Bell, 1954.

Lévi-Strauss, Claude. *Anthropologie structurale*. Paris: Plon, 1958.

Anthropologie structurale deux. Paris: Plon, 1973.

The Elementary Structures of Kinship. Translated by John Richard Von Sturmer, James Harle Bell, and Rodney Needham. Boston, MA: Beacon Press, 1969.

Mythologiques vols. 1–4:

Le Cru et le cuit. Paris: Plon, 1964.

The Raw and the Cooked. Translated by John Weightman and Doreen Weightman. New York: Harper & Row, 1969.

Du Miel aux cendres. Paris: Plon, 1966.

From Honey to Ashes. Translated by John Weightman and Doreen Weightman. New York: Harper & Row, 1973.

L'Origine des manières de table. Paris: Plon, 1968.

The Origin of Table Manners. Translated by John Weightman and Doreen Weightman. New York: Harper & Row, 1978.

L'Homme nu. Paris, Plon, 1971.

The Naked Man. Translated by John Weightman and Doreen Weightman. New York: Harper & Row, 1981.

La Pensée sauvage. Paris: Plon, 1962.

The Sad Tropics. Translated by John Russell. London: Hutchinson & Co., 1961.

The Savage Mind. Chicago: University of Chicago Press, 1966.

"Structural Analysis in Linguistics and in Anthropology." *Word* 1, no. 2 (1945): 1–12.

Structural Anthropology. Translated by Claire Jacobson and Brooke Grundfest Schoepf. New York: Basic Books, 1963.

Les Structures élémentaires de la parenté. Paris: Presses universitaires de France, 1949.

Totemism. Translated by R. Needham. Boston: Beacon Press, 1963.

Le Totémisme aujourd'hui. Paris: Presses universitaires de France, 1962.

Tristes Tropiques. Paris, Plon, 1955.

La Vie familiale et sociale des indiens Nambikwara. Paris: Au siège de la société, Musée de l'Homme, 1948.

Lowie, Robert H. *Primitive Society*. New York: Liveright Pub. Corp., 1947.

Mandelbaum, David. "Myths and Myth Maker: Some Anthropological Appraisals of the Mythological Studies of Lévi-Strauss." *Ethnology* 26, no. 1 (January 1987): 31–6.

Radcliffe-Brown, A. R. "The Comparative Method in Social Anthropology." *Journal of the Royal Anthropological Institute of Great Britain and Ireland* 81, no. 1/2 (1951): 15–22.

"On Social Structure." *Journal of the Royal Anthropological Institute of Great Britain and Ireland* 70, no. 1 (1940): 1–12.

Remington, Alexander F. "Renowned Anthropologist Claude Lévi-Strauss Dies at 100." *Washington Post,* November 5, 2009. Accessed January 29, 2016. http://www.washingtonpost.com/wp-dyn/content/article/2009/11/03/AR2009110301477.html.

Richman, Michèle. "Review of *Claude Lévi-Strauss and the Making of Structural Anthropology* by Marcel Hénaff." *SubStance* 29, no. 3 issue 93: special issue: Pierre Bourdieu (2000): 132–4.

Rodinson, Maxime. "Ethnographie et relativisme." *La Nouvelle Critique* 69 (1955): 49–63.

Rohlf, Michael. "Immanuel Kant." In *Stanford Encyclopedia of Philosophy*. Accessed February 1, 2016. http://plato.stanford.edu/entries/kant/.

Sahlins, Marshall. "On the Anthropology of Levi-Strauss." American Anthropological Association blog, July 7, 2009. Accessed February 2, 2016. http://blog.americananthro.org/2009/07/07/on-the-anthropology-of-levi-strauss/.

de Saussure, Ferdinand. *Course in General Linguistics*. Translated by Roy Harris. London: Duckworth, 2013.

Écrits de linguistique générale. Paris: Gallimard, 2002.

Smith, Claire, ed. *Encyclopedia of Global Archaeology*, 11 vols. New York: Springer-Verlag, 2014.

Sontag, Susan. *Against Interpretation: And Other Essays.* New York: Farrar, Straus and Giroux, 1966.

"A Hero of Our Time." *New York Review of Books*. November 28, 1963.

Tilley, Chris Y. "Claude Lévi-Strauss: Structuralism and Beyond." In *Reading Material Culture*, edited by C. Y. Tilley, 3–81. Cambridge, MA: Blackwell, 1990.

Trigger, Bruce. *A History of Archaeological Thought*. New York: Cambridge University Press, 1989.

Wilcken, Patrick. *Claude Lévi-Strauss: The Father of Modern Anthropology.* London: Penguin Books, 2010.

Willey, Gordon and Philip Phillips. *Method and Theory in American Archaeology*. Chicago: University of Chicago Press, 1958.

World Economics Association. "Interview on Neo-structuralism." World Economics Association website. Accessed February 2, 2016, http://www.worldeconomicsassociation.org/newsletterarticles/neo-structuralism/.

THE MACAT LIBRARY
BY DISCIPLINE

AFRICANA STUDIES

Chinua Achebe's *An Image of Africa: Racism in Conrad's Heart of Darkness*
W. E. B. Du Bois's *The Souls of Black Folk*
Zora Neale Huston's *Characteristics of Negro Expression*
Martin Luther King Jr's *Why We Can't Wait*
Toni Morrison's *Playing in the Dark: Whiteness in the American Literary Imagination*

ANTHROPOLOGY

Arjun Appadurai's *Modernity at Large: Cultural Dimensions of Globalisation*
Philippe Ariès's *Centuries of Childhood*
Franz Boas's *Race, Language and Culture*
Kim Chan & Renée Mauborgne's *Blue Ocean Strategy*
Jared Diamond's *Guns, Germs & Steel: the Fate of Human Societies*
Jared Diamond's *Collapse: How Societies Choose to Fail or Survive*
E. E. Evans-Pritchard's *Witchcraft, Oracles and Magic Among the Azande*
James Ferguson's *The Anti-Politics Machine*
Clifford Geertz's *The Interpretation of Cultures*
David Graeber's *Debt: the First 5000 Years*
Karen Ho's *Liquidated: An Ethnography of Wall Street*
Geert Hofstede's *Culture's Consequences: Comparing Values, Behaviors, Institutes and Organizations across Nations*
Claude Lévi-Strauss's *Structural Anthropology*
Jay Macleod's *Ain't No Makin' It: Aspirations and Attainment in a Low-Income Neighborhood*
Saba Mahmood's *The Politics of Piety: The Islamic Revival and the Feminist Subject*
Marcel Mauss's *The Gift*

BUSINESS

Jean Lave & Etienne Wenger's *Situated Learning*
Theodore Levitt's *Marketing Myopia*
Burton G. Malkiel's *A Random Walk Down Wall Street*
Douglas McGregor's *The Human Side of Enterprise*
Michael Porter's *Competitive Strategy: Creating and Sustaining Superior Performance*
John Kotter's *Leading Change*
C. K. Prahalad & Gary Hamel's *The Core Competence of the Corporation*

CRIMINOLOGY

Michelle Alexander's *The New Jim Crow: Mass Incarceration in the Age of Colorblindness*
Michael R. Gottfredson & Travis Hirschi's *A General Theory of Crime*
Richard Herrnstein & Charles A. Murray's *The Bell Curve: Intelligence and Class Structure in American Life*
Elizabeth Loftus's *Eyewitness Testimony*
Jay Macleod's *Ain't No Makin' It: Aspirations and Attainment in a Low-Income Neighborhood*
Philip Zimbardo's *The Lucifer Effect*

ECONOMICS

Janet Abu-Lughod's *Before European Hegemony*
Ha-Joon Chang's *Kicking Away the Ladder*
David Brion Davis's *The Problem of Slavery in the Age of Revolution*
Milton Friedman's *The Role of Monetary Policy*
Milton Friedman's *Capitalism and Freedom*
David Graeber's *Debt: the First 5000 Years*
Friedrich Hayek's *The Road to Serfdom*
Karen Ho's *Liquidated: An Ethnography of Wall Street*

The Macat Library By Discipline

John Maynard Keynes's *The General Theory of Employment, Interest and Money*
Charles P. Kindleberger's *Manias, Panics and Crashes*
Robert Lucas's *Why Doesn't Capital Flow from Rich to Poor Countries?*
Burton G. Malkiel's *A Random Walk Down Wall Street*
Thomas Robert Malthus's *An Essay on the Principle of Population*
Karl Marx's *Capital*
Thomas Piketty's *Capital in the Twenty-First Century*
Amartya Sen's *Development as Freedom*
Adam Smith's *The Wealth of Nations*
Nassim Nicholas Taleb's *The Black Swan: The Impact of the Highly Improbable*
Amos Tversky's & Daniel Kahneman's *Judgment under Uncertainty: Heuristics and Biases*
Mahbub Ul Haq's *Reflections on Human Development*
Max Weber's *The Protestant Ethic and the Spirit of Capitalism*

FEMINISM AND GENDER STUDIES

Judith Butler's *Gender Trouble*
Simone De Beauvoir's *The Second Sex*
Michel Foucault's *History of Sexuality*
Betty Friedan's *The Feminine Mystique*
Saba Mahmood's *The Politics of Piety: The Islamic Revival and the Feminist Subject*
Joan Wallach Scott's *Gender and the Politics of History*
Mary Wollstonecraft's *A Vindication of the Rights of Woman*
Virginia Woolf's *A Room of One's Own*

GEOGRAPHY

The Brundtland Report's *Our Common Future*
Rachel Carson's *Silent Spring*
Charles Darwin's *On the Origin of Species*
James Ferguson's *The Anti-Politics Machine*
Jane Jacobs's *The Death and Life of Great American Cities*
James Lovelock's *Gaia: A New Look at Life on Earth*
Amartya Sen's *Development as Freedom*
Mathis Wackernagel & William Rees's *Our Ecological Footprint*

HISTORY

Janet Abu-Lughod's *Before European Hegemony*
Benedict Anderson's *Imagined Communities*
Bernard Bailyn's *The Ideological Origins of the American Revolution*
Hanna Batatu's *The Old Social Classes And The Revolutionary Movements Of Iraq*
Christopher Browning's *Ordinary Men: Reserve Police Batallion 101 and the Final Solution in Poland*
Edmund Burke's *Reflections on the Revolution in France*
William Cronon's *Nature's Metropolis: Chicago And The Great West*
Alfred W. Crosby's *The Columbian Exchange*
Hamid Dabashi's *Iran: A People Interrupted*
David Brion Davis's *The Problem of Slavery in the Age of Revolution*
Nathalie Zemon Davis's *The Return of Martin Guerre*
Jared Diamond's *Guns, Germs & Steel: the Fate of Human Societies*
Frank Dikotter's *Mao's Great Famine*
John W Dower's *War Without Mercy: Race And Power In The Pacific War*
W. E. B. Du Bois's *The Souls of Black Folk*
Richard J. Evans's *In Defence of History*
Lucien Febvre's *The Problem of Unbelief in the 16th Century*
Sheila Fitzpatrick's *Everyday Stalinism*

Eric Foner's *Reconstruction: America's Unfinished Revolution, 1863-1877*
Michel Foucault's *Discipline and Punish*
Michel Foucault's *History of Sexuality*
Francis Fukuyama's *The End of History and the Last Man*
John Lewis Gaddis's *We Now Know: Rethinking Cold War History*
Ernest Gellner's *Nations and Nationalism*
Eugene Genovese's *Roll, Jordan, Roll: The World the Slaves Made*
Carlo Ginzburg's *The Night Battles*
Daniel Goldhagen's *Hitler's Willing Executioners*
Jack Goldstone's *Revolution and Rebellion in the Early Modern World*
Antonio Gramsci's *The Prison Notebooks*
Alexander Hamilton, John Jay & James Madison's *The Federalist Papers*
Christopher Hill's *The World Turned Upside Down*
Carole Hillenbrand's *The Crusades: Islamic Perspectives*
Thomas Hobbes's *Leviathan*
Eric Hobsbawm's *The Age Of Revolution*
John A. Hobson's *Imperialism: A Study*
Albert Hourani's *History of the Arab Peoples*
Samuel P. Huntington's *The Clash of Civilizations and the Remaking of World Order*
C. L. R. James's *The Black Jacobins*
Tony Judt's *Postwar: A History of Europe Since 1945*
Ernst Kantorowicz's *The King's Two Bodies: A Study in Medieval Political Theology*
Paul Kennedy's *The Rise and Fall of the Great Powers*
Ian Kershaw's *The "Hitler Myth": Image and Reality in the Third Reich*
John Maynard Keynes's *The General Theory of Employment, Interest and Money*
Charles P. Kindleberger's *Manias, Panics and Crashes*
Martin Luther King Jr's *Why We Can't Wait*
Henry Kissinger's *World Order: Reflections on the Character of Nations and the Course of History*
Thomas Kuhn's *The Structure of Scientific Revolutions*
Georges Lefebvre's *The Coming of the French Revolution*
John Locke's *Two Treatises of Government*
Niccolò Machiavelli's *The Prince*
Thomas Robert Malthus's *An Essay on the Principle of Population*
Mahmood Mamdani's *Citizen and Subject: Contemporary Africa And The Legacy Of Late Colonialism*
Karl Marx's *Capital*
Stanley Milgram's *Obedience to Authority*
John Stuart Mill's *On Liberty*
Thomas Paine's *Common Sense*
Thomas Paine's *Rights of Man*
Geoffrey Parker's *Global Crisis: War, Climate Change and Catastrophe in the Seventeenth Century*
Jonathan Riley-Smith's *The First Crusade and the Idea of Crusading*
Jean-Jacques Rousseau's *The Social Contract*
Joan Wallach Scott's *Gender and the Politics of History*
Theda Skocpol's *States and Social Revolutions*
Adam Smith's *The Wealth of Nations*
Timothy Snyder's *Bloodlands: Europe Between Hitler and Stalin*
Sun Tzu's *The Art of War*
Keith Thomas's *Religion and the Decline of Magic*
Thucydides's *The History of the Peloponnesian War*
Frederick Jackson Turner's *The Significance of the Frontier in American History*
Odd Arne Westad's *The Global Cold War: Third World Interventions And The Making Of Our Times*

The Macat Library By Discipline

LITERATURE

Chinua Achebe's *An Image of Africa: Racism in Conrad's Heart of Darkness*
Roland Barthes's *Mythologies*
Homi K. Bhabha's *The Location of Culture*
Judith Butler's *Gender Trouble*
Simone De Beauvoir's *The Second Sex*
Ferdinand De Saussure's *Course in General Linguistics*
T. S. Eliot's *The Sacred Wood: Essays on Poetry and Criticism*
Zora Neale Huston's *Characteristics of Negro Expression*
Toni Morrison's *Playing in the Dark: Whiteness in the American Literary Imagination*
Edward Said's *Orientalism*
Gayatri Chakravorty Spivak's *Can the Subaltern Speak?*
Mary Wollstonecraft's *A Vindication of the Rights of Women*
Virginia Woolf's *A Room of One's Own*

PHILOSOPHY

Elizabeth Anscombe's *Modern Moral Philosophy*
Hannah Arendt's *The Human Condition*
Aristotle's *Metaphysics*
Aristotle's *Nicomachean Ethics*
Edmund Gettier's *Is Justified True Belief Knowledge?*
Georg Wilhelm Friedrich Hegel's *Phenomenology of Spirit*
David Hume's *Dialogues Concerning Natural Religion*
David Hume's *The Enquiry for Human Understanding*
Immanuel Kant's *Religion within the Boundaries of Mere Reason*
Immanuel Kant's *Critique of Pure Reason*
Søren Kierkegaard's *The Sickness Unto Death*
Søren Kierkegaard's *Fear and Trembling*
C. S. Lewis's *The Abolition of Man*
Alasdair MacIntyre's *After Virtue*
Marcus Aurelius's *Meditations*
Friedrich Nietzsche's *On the Genealogy of Morality*
Friedrich Nietzsche's *Beyond Good and Evil*
Plato's *Republic*
Plato's *Symposium*
Jean-Jacques Rousseau's *The Social Contract*
Gilbert Ryle's *The Concept of Mind*
Baruch Spinoza's *Ethics*
Sun Tzu's *The Art of War*
Ludwig Wittgenstein's *Philosophical Investigations*

POLITICS

Benedict Anderson's *Imagined Communities*
Aristotle's *Politics*
Bernard Bailyn's *The Ideological Origins of the American Revolution*
Edmund Burke's *Reflections on the Revolution in France*
John C. Calhoun's *A Disquisition on Government*
Ha-Joon Chang's *Kicking Away the Ladder*
Hamid Dabashi's *Iran: A People Interrupted*
Hamid Dabashi's *Theology of Discontent: The Ideological Foundation of the Islamic Revolution in Iran*
Robert Dahl's *Democracy and its Critics*
Robert Dahl's *Who Governs?*
David Brion Davis's *The Problem of Slavery in the Age of Revolution*

Alexis De Tocqueville's *Democracy in America*
James Ferguson's *The Anti-Politics Machine*
Frank Dikotter's *Mao's Great Famine*
Sheila Fitzpatrick's *Everyday Stalinism*
Eric Foner's *Reconstruction: America's Unfinished Revolution, 1863-1877*
Milton Friedman's *Capitalism and Freedom*
Francis Fukuyama's *The End of History and the Last Man*
John Lewis Gaddis's *We Now Know: Rethinking Cold War History*
Ernest Gellner's *Nations and Nationalism*
David Graeber's *Debt: the First 5000 Years*
Antonio Gramsci's *The Prison Notebooks*
Alexander Hamilton, John Jay & James Madison's *The Federalist Papers*
Friedrich Hayek's *The Road to Serfdom*
Christopher Hill's *The World Turned Upside Down*
Thomas Hobbes's *Leviathan*
John A. Hobson's *Imperialism: A Study*
Samuel P. Huntington's *The Clash of Civilizations and the Remaking of World Order*
Tony Judt's *Postwar: A History of Europe Since 1945*
David C. Kang's *China Rising: Peace, Power and Order in East Asia*
Paul Kennedy's *The Rise and Fall of Great Powers*
Robert Keohane's *After Hegemony*
Martin Luther King Jr.'s *Why We Can't Wait*
Henry Kissinger's *World Order: Reflections on the Character of Nations and the Course of History*
John Locke's *Two Treatises of Government*
Niccolò Machiavelli's *The Prince*
Thomas Robert Malthus's *An Essay on the Principle of Population*
Mahmood Mamdani's *Citizen and Subject: Contemporary Africa And The Legacy Of
Late Colonialism*
Karl Marx's *Capital*
John Stuart Mill's *On Liberty*
John Stuart Mill's *Utilitarianism*
Hans Morgenthau's *Politics Among Nations*
Thomas Paine's *Common Sense*
Thomas Paine's *Rights of Man*
Thomas Piketty's *Capital in the Twenty-First Century*
Robert D. Putman's *Bowling Alone*
John Rawls's *Theory of Justice*
Jean-Jacques Rousseau's *The Social Contract*
Theda Skocpol's *States and Social Revolutions*
Adam Smith's *The Wealth of Nations*
Sun Tzu's *The Art of War*
Henry David Thoreau's *Civil Disobedience*
Thucydides's *The History of the Peloponnesian War*
Kenneth Waltz's *Theory of International Politics*
Max Weber's *Politics as a Vocation*
Odd Arne Westad's *The Global Cold War: Third World Interventions And The Making Of Our Times*

POSTCOLONIAL STUDIES

Roland Barthes's *Mythologies*
Frantz Fanon's *Black Skin, White Masks*
Homi K. Bhabha's *The Location of Culture*
Gustavo Gutiérrez's *A Theology of Liberation*
Edward Said's *Orientalism*
Gayatri Chakravorty Spivak's *Can the Subaltern Speak?*

The Macat Library By Discipline

PSYCHOLOGY

Gordon Allport's *The Nature of Prejudice*
Alan Baddeley & Graham Hitch's *Aggression: A Social Learning Analysis*
Albert Bandura's *Aggression: A Social Learning Analysis*
Leon Festinger's *A Theory of Cognitive Dissonance*
Sigmund Freud's *The Interpretation of Dreams*
Betty Friedan's *The Feminine Mystique*
Michael R. Gottfredson & Travis Hirschi's *A General Theory of Crime*
Eric Hoffer's *The True Believer: Thoughts on the Nature of Mass Movements*
William James's *Principles of Psychology*
Elizabeth Loftus's *Eyewitness Testimony*
A. H. Maslow's *A Theory of Human Motivation*
Stanley Milgram's *Obedience to Authority*
Steven Pinker's *The Better Angels of Our Nature*
Oliver Sacks's *The Man Who Mistook His Wife For a Hat*
Richard Thaler & Cass Sunstein's *Nudge: Improving Decisions About Health, Wealth and Happiness*
Amos Tversky's *Judgment under Uncertainty: Heuristics and Biases*
Philip Zimbardo's *The Lucifer Effect*

SCIENCE

Rachel Carson's *Silent Spring*
William Cronon's *Nature's Metropolis: Chicago And The Great West*
Alfred W. Crosby's *The Columbian Exchange*
Charles Darwin's *On the Origin of Species*
Richard Dawkin's *The Selfish Gene*
Thomas Kuhn's *The Structure of Scientific Revolutions*
Geoffrey Parker's *Global Crisis: War, Climate Change and Catastrophe in the Seventeenth Century*
Mathis Wackernagel & William Rees's *Our Ecological Footprint*

SOCIOLOGY

Michelle Alexander's *The New Jim Crow: Mass Incarceration in the Age of Colorblindness*
Gordon Allport's *The Nature of Prejudice*
Albert Bandura's *Aggression: A Social Learning Analysis*
Hanna Batatu's *The Old Social Classes And The Revolutionary Movements Of Iraq*
Ha-Joon Chang's *Kicking Away the Ladder*
W. E. B. Du Bois's *The Souls of Black Folk*
Émile Durkheim's *On Suicide*
Frantz Fanon's *Black Skin, White Masks*
Frantz Fanon's *The Wretched of the Earth*
Eric Foner's *Reconstruction: America's Unfinished Revolution, 1863-1877*
Eugene Genovese's *Roll, Jordan, Roll: The World the Slaves Made*
Jack Goldstone's *Revolution and Rebellion in the Early Modern World*
Antonio Gramsci's *The Prison Notebooks*
Richard Herrnstein & Charles A Murray's *The Bell Curve: Intelligence and Class Structure in American Life*
Eric Hoffer's *The True Believer: Thoughts on the Nature of Mass Movements*
Jane Jacobs's *The Death and Life of Great American Cities*
Robert Lucas's *Why Doesn't Capital Flow from Rich to Poor Countries?*
Jay Macleod's *Ain't No Makin' It: Aspirations and Attainment in a Low Income Neighborhood*
Elaine May's *Homeward Bound: American Families in the Cold War Era*
Douglas McGregor's *The Human Side of Enterprise*
C. Wright Mills's *The Sociological Imagination*

Thomas Piketty's *Capital in the Twenty-First Century*
Robert D. Putman's *Bowling Alone*
David Riesman's *The Lonely Crowd: A Study of the Changing American Character*
Edward Said's *Orientalism*
Joan Wallach Scott's *Gender and the Politics of History*
Theda Skocpol's *States and Social Revolutions*
Max Weber's *The Protestant Ethic and the Spirit of Capitalism*

THEOLOGY

Augustine's *Confessions*
Benedict's *Rule of St Benedict*
Gustavo Gutiérrez's *A Theology of Liberation*
Carole Hillenbrand's *The Crusades: Islamic Perspectives*
David Hume's *Dialogues Concerning Natural Religion*
Immanuel Kant's *Religion within the Boundaries of Mere Reason*
Ernst Kantorowicz's *The King's Two Bodies: A Study in Medieval Political Theology*
Søren Kierkegaard's *The Sickness Unto Death*
C. S. Lewis's *The Abolition of Man*
Saba Mahmood's *The Politics of Piety: The Islamic Revival and the Feminist Subjec*t
Baruch Spinoza's *Ethics*
Keith Thomas's *Religion and the Decline of Magic*

COMING SOON

Chris Argyris's *The Individual and the Organisation*
Seyla Benhabib's *The Rights of Others*
Walter Benjamin's *The Work Of Art in the Age of Mechanical Reproduction*
John Berger's *Ways of Seeing*
Pierre Bourdieu's *Outline of a Theory of Practice*
Mary Douglas's *Purity and Danger*
Roland Dworkin's *Taking Rights Seriously*
James G. March's *Exploration and Exploitation in Organisational Learning*
Ikujiro Nonaka's *A Dynamic Theory of Organizational Knowledge Creation*
Griselda Pollock's *Vision and Difference*
Amartya Sen's *Inequality Re-Examined*
Susan Sontag's *On Photography*
Yasser Tabbaa's *The Transformation of Islamic Art*
Ludwig von Mises's *Theory of Money and Credit*

Macat Disciplines

Access the greatest ideas and thinkers across entire disciplines, including

TOTALITARIANISM

Sheila Fitzpatrick's, *Everyday Stalinism*
Ian Kershaw's, *The "Hitler Myth"*
Timothy Snyder's, *Bloodlands*

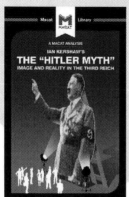

Macat Pairs

Analyse historical and modern issues from opposite sides of an argument. Pairs include:

RACE AND IDENTITY

Zora Neale Hurston's
Characteristics of Negro Expression

Using material collected on anthropological expeditions to the South, Zora Neale Hurston explains how expression in African American culture in the early twentieth century departs from the art of white America. At the time, African American art was often criticized for copying white culture. For Hurston, this criticism misunderstood how art works. European tradition views art as something fixed. But Hurston describes a creative process that is alive, ever-changing, and largely improvisational. She maintains that African American art works through a process called 'mimicry'—where an imitated object or verbal pattern, for example, is reshaped and altered until it becomes something new, novel—and worthy of attention.

Frantz Fanon's
Black Skin, White Masks

Black Skin, White Masks offers a radical analysis of the psychological effects of colonization on the colonized.

Fanon witnessed the effects of colonization first hand both in his birthplace, Martinique, and again later in life when he worked as a psychiatrist in another French colony, Algeria. His text is uncompromising in form and argument. He dissects the dehumanizing effects of colonialism, arguing that it destroys the native sense of identity, forcing people to adapt to an alien set of values—including a core belief that they are inferior. This results in deep psychological trauma.

Fanon's work played a pivotal role in the civil rights movements of the 1960s.

Macat analyses are available from all good bookshops and libraries.

Access hundreds of analyses through one, multimedia tool.
Join free for one month **library.macat.com**

Macat Pairs

*Analyse historical and modern issues
from opposite sides of an argument.
Pairs include:*

INTERNATIONAL RELATIONS IN THE 21ˢᵀ CENTURY

Samuel P. Huntington's
The Clash of Civilisations

In his highly influential 1996 book, Huntington offers a vision of a post-Cold War world in which conflict takes place not between competing ideologies but between cultures. The worst clash, he argues, will be between the Islamic world and the West: the West's arrogance and belief that its culture is a "gift" to the world will come into conflict with Islam's obstinacy and concern that its culture is under attack from a morally decadent "other."

Clash inspired much debate between different political schools of thought. But its greatest impact came in helping define American foreign policy in the wake of the 2001 terrorist attacks in New York and Washington.

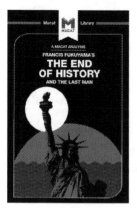

Francis Fukuyama's
The End of History and the Last Man

Published in 1992, *The End of History and the Last Man* argues that capitalist democracy is the final destination for all societies. Fukuyama believed democracy triumphed during the Cold War because it lacks the "fundamental contradictions" inherent in communism and satisfies our yearning for freedom and equality. Democracy therefore marks the endpoint in the evolution of ideology, and so the "end of history." There will still be "events," but no fundamental change in ideology.

Printed in the United States
by Baker & Taylor Publisher Services

Macat Disciplines

Access the greatest ideas and thinkers across entire disciplines, including

MAN AND THE ENVIRONMENT

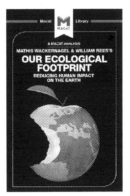

The Brundtland Report's, *Our Common Future*
Rachel Carson's, *Silent Spring*
James Lovelock's, *Gaia: A New Look at Life on Earth*
Mathis Wackernagel & William Rees's, *Our Ecological Footprint*

Macat analyses are available from all good bookshops and libraries.

Access hundreds of analyses through one, multimedia tool.
Join free for one month **library.macat.com**